Editor's Preface

In terms of the effect on other people, the management of complex enterprises, in business, in government, and in the military services is certainly the most important activity in which individual men engage. Sound and imaginative management can fashion a successful and useful enterprise out of routine materials, while poor management can vitiate the most brilliant technical and staff work and lead to an appalling waste of human effort.

Despite its importance, management is one of the most recent fields to seek assistance from the formal apparatus of science. Some of the tools used in management science—time and motion study, for example—have existed for some time. The application of scientific methods to a whole management problem, rather than merely to the gathering of data, seems to have gotten underway only during and after World War II, however. The feature that distinguishes the new approach is that a problem and the system that generates the problem are initially described in the most general terms possible, in order that the widest range of possible models can be studied and the widest range of possible solutions surveyed.

Management science is not a theoretician's exercise, however. The problems are intensely practical and must be solved in real time. Much of the value of this book derives from the fact that the author has been able to include a number of examples from his own experience as a practicing management scientist.

Management Science

The Business Use of Operations Research

Stafford Beer

Doubleday Science Series
Doubleday & Company, Inc.
Garden City, New York, 1968

First Published in the United States of America in 1967 by
Doubleday & Company, Inc., Garden City, New York
In Association with Aldus Books Limited
Library of Congress Catalog Card No. 67-10551
Copyright © Aldus Books Limited, London, 1967
Printed in Italy by Arnoldo Mondadori, Verona

Contents

Suggested Reading

By Stafford Beer:

Decision and Control, John Wiley (London, 1966)

Cybernetics and Management, English Universities Press (London, 1959)

Classics on Operations Research

P. M. Morse & G. E. Kimball, *Methods of Operations Research*, Technology Press of M.I.T. and John Wiley (New York, revised edition 1951).

J. F. McCloskey & F. N. Trefethen, *Operations Research for Management*, Johns Hopkins Press (Baltimore, 1954).

C. W. Churchman, R. L. Ackoff, and E. L. Arnoff, *Introduction to Operations Research*, John Wiley (New York, 1957).

General Works on Operations Research

C. W. Churchman, *Prediction and Optional Decision*, Prentice Hall (New Jersey 1961).

R. T. Eddison, K. Pennycuick, and B. H. P. Rivett, *Operational Research in Management*, John Wiley (New York), 1962.

C. D. Flagle, W. H. Huggins, and R. H. Roy, *Operations Research and Systems Engineering*, Johns Hopkins Press (Baltimore, 1960).

H. A. Simon, *Models of Man*, John Wiley (New York, 1957).

J. D. Williams, *The Compleat Strategist*, McGraw Hill (New York, 1954).

Conferences and Series

Proceedings of the First (1957), *Second* (1960), *and Third* (1963) *International Conferences on Operational Research*, English Universities Press.

Progress in Operations Research Vol. 1 (Ed. Ackoff), 1961, Vol. II (Eds. D. B. Hertz and R. T. Eddison), John Wiley (New York, 1964).

Introductory Cybernetics

W. Ross Ashby, *An Introduction to Cybernetics*, John Wiley (New York, 1956).

G. Pask, *An Approach to Cybernetics*, Harper and Row (New York, 1962).

E. A. Feigenbaum & J. Feldman (Eds.), *Computers and Thought*, McGraw Hill (San Francisco, 1964).

Acknowledgments

Page 11 Courtesy Yuri Gridneff; photo B. Kapadia: 12 Mansell Collection: 13 Photo Media Associates: 14 Mansell Collection: 15 Metropolitan Museum of Art, New York: 17 Photo M. Buselle: 18 Photo B. Kapadia: 21 British Crown Copyright: 23 Imperial War Museum: 30 *Motor Sport*: 33 Photo B. Kapadia: 55 Photo M. Buselle: 59 *Illustrated London News*: 60 London Transport Executive: 68 Glaxo Laboratories Ltd.: 71 Imperial Chemical Industries Ltd.: 88 (Top) Rover Co. Ltd. (Bottom) Photo B. Kapadia: 90 Scientific American Inc.: 95 From the film *Amoeba* distributed by Rank Film Library: 99 Based on C. U. M. Smith, *The Architecture of the Body*, Cambridge University Press: 102 (Top) Photo D. McCullin (Bottom) English Electric Co. Ltd.: 104 Photo *Paris Match*: 111 Photomicrograph Gene Cox: 121 Photo R. Nelson: 140 Photo B. Kapadia: 142 Robert R. Goller, *Civil Engineering* A.S.C.E. 1965: 152 Photo Novak/Barnaby: 164 United Features Syndicate: 165 Photo Bill Rogers: 168 From *Histoires des Inventions*, Editions du Pont Royal, Paris: 171 Mansell Collection: 172 (Top) Courtesy Raleigh Industries; Photo John Isaac (Bottom) Drummond Asquith Ltd.: 177 Photo B. Kapadia: 186 Decca Navigator Co. Ltd.: 189 Courtesy *Tutorage*, U.S. Industries Inc. (Great Britain) Ltd.

1 Processes and Policies

How do people manage to manage? The answer seems evident: by knowledge and experience. To be a manager is not the same thing as to be a leader, although leadership is a quality too often underrated in modern management. There are indeed many aspects of the manager's job that depend on his character—on determination, on drive, on flair. But the tasks of management are undeniably intellectual tasks.

First of all, a manager has to formulate a policy. He always works within the framework of a policy handed to him by someone else: perhaps by the board, or if he is himself a member of the board, then by the government that sets the context of the manager's enterprise. It remains a fact, however, that to do his own job, he must himself create a policy at some appropriate level.

Secondly, the manager must take decisions within the framework of policy. In the public mind, there seems to be something dramatic about taking a decision. I suppose this is because the decisions one normally hears of in the news are attended by drama. In everyday life, on the contrary, the manager's day incorporates many decisions that appear dull and prosaic, but that nevertheless sum up to the success or failure of the affairs for which he is responsible.

Thirdly, the manager who formulates policy and takes decisions within it achieves nothing at all without some machinery for implementation. Probably this machinery exists independently of him: He inherits a staff, he inherits services, he inherits a going concern when he takes on the job. But the way in which he operates this machinery is his affair. He may be served with figures, and not know how to use them. He may so alienate a subordinate manager that he never receives that man's full support. In short, he has to take personal responsibility for the mode of control he exercises.

Policy-making, decision-taking, and control: These are the three functions of management that have intellectual content. A man may be very good at any two of them, and still make a hash of his job for want of capability with the third. And whatever can be said for the qualities of drive and leadership, which is a lot, these attributes cannot in the long run be expected to compensate for deficiencies in the three-pronged intellectual attack.

An Art, Yes, But a Science Too
As I was saying, then, managers manage to manage by knowledge and experience. This means to say that they rely on their knowledge of the business, and of businesses in general, to tell them what policies to formulate and what decisions to contemplate. It is experience, above all, that teaches them how to control. No wonder people say that management is an art. It is.

By the same token, of course, shipbuilding is an art. For a good many thousand years, men built ships from a knowledge of the way hollowed-out vessels behave when tossed about on water, and became wise in this pursuit from continual experience too. Yet today there is more to shipbuilding than used to be passed from father to son. The factors involved have been *codified*, and built into a teachable whole as well: New ideas may be systematically tested against it, new discoveries may be fitted into it. It is this codification and summation of knowledge and experience that we call science.

By far the best definition of science I know is: systematic knowledge about the world. And of course science applies to other things than shipbuilding. By building up a codified knowledge of what experience teaches, man has acquired a body of knowledge that can be communicated. That is the whole point about the

A manager who excels in drive and leadership but is not skilled in the three intellectual functions of management may be compared to a man on a unicycle—the unicyclist gives a virtuoso display over the short term, but a delivery boy on a tricycle will make steadier progress and carry a more useful load.

codification. Instead of passing on information from generation to generation, and from one craftsman to another, by a process of imitated action and by a mystique of unexplained hints and wrinkles, science distils all that wisdom into something more pithy. Codification incorporates the notions of *coherence* and of *rigor* and of *pattern*. Essentially it is all aimed at better communication, both as to how knowledge may be transmitted and as to what insight there is to transmit.

As a result, a young man can go to college and be taught a very large proportion of the total wisdom of mankind in relation to a craft such as shipbuilding in a few years. And he may learn not only practical techniques in this way; he may also acquire a large proportion of man's knowledge of physics or of chemistry or of biology by these means. When he has finished the course, he will still be—as we say—green. There is a lot more to learn about what all this means in practice. There is a gap between knowledge and wisdom. But the young man has a flying start.

When it comes to the business of management, however, there is a strange silence. It is not generally agreed that there *is* such a subject as management science, nor is there unanimous support for the idea that management can at all be taught. The most obvious reason for this would be that no one has managed to codify the experience mankind has had of managing things. But surely that stage ought to be reached? This book will try to persuade you that it has been reached.

Let us get the claim right from the outset. To say that there can be a science of management is not to deny that management is an art. The man with the genius for designing buildings is not less of an artist because he is a competent architect. It is a very good thing for us all that he is. Secondly, we should not confuse the contention that there can be a systematic knowledge of management with the notion that there are particular techniques, used by managers, that can be taught. This is a mistake that, it seems to me, is often made

An individual statue is a work of art, but systematic scientific principles are used to achieve a sense of action from a static object, even to make it stand up.

The belief that management is a teachable science is expressed in the numerous schools and colleges that specialize in the subject. An early example was the Harvard Business School, the library of which is seen here.

in very high quarters. We know that managers ought to be able to read a balance sheet, to understand costings, and so forth, and obviously these are particular skills that can be communicated. But the claim that there is a management science, if it is to be upheld at all, cannot be made out like that. The science of a subject is always about its very nature; it is not about virtuosity.

Most science began as a body of esoteric knowledge—that is, it was known only to a few. Inevitably, mystery surrounded the subject; communication was barred to outsiders by the use of peculiar languages, and the transmission of what was known depended on a supply of apprentices who were inducted into the cult. Indeed, the whole of science was once in this stage, in the hands of the alchemists. Typically, anyone who alleged that the body of knowledge concerned could be codified in an objective way

14

The alchemists' symbols, shown here with their modern equivalents, served as much to conceal information from outsiders as to convey it to those who could read them.

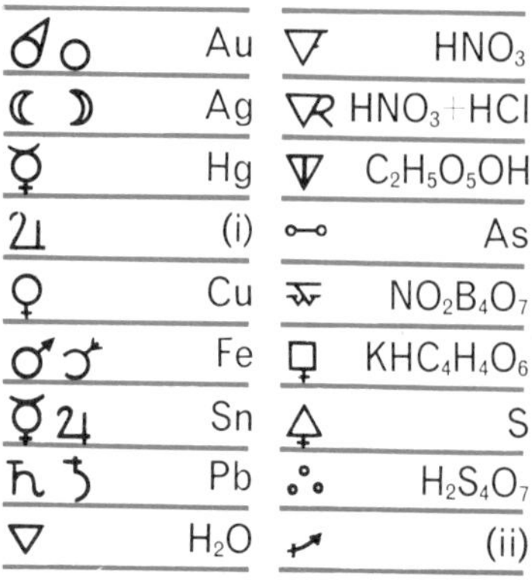

♂o	Au	▽	HNO_3
☾ ☽	Ag	℞	$HNO_3 + HCl$
☿	Hg	⩔	$C_2H_5O_5OH$
♃	(i)	o—o	As
♀	Cu	�"⊽"	$NO_2B_4O_7$
♂♂	Fe	⎍	$KHC_4H_4O_6$
☿♃	Sn	⌔	S
♄ ☽	Pb	°.°	$H_2S_4O_7$
▽	H_2O	⤴	(ii)

The attitude of the scientist is expressed in Lord Kelvin's dictum, "Whatever exists, exists in some quantity, and can therefore be measured."

The beginnings of science in Egypt were measurements in connection with irrigation.

for general communication was treated roughly. But intellect usually triumphs in the end. And today we recognize that a body of knowledge has become a science by certain marks. First of all, things are measured. Secondly, only things that result in the same measurement many times by many observers count as facts. Thirdly, hypotheses are formed to account for the facts being as they are, and these hypotheses are tested in every way that anyone can think of. Next, a hypothesis that does not break down after continuous testing over the years acquires the status of a " law." Finally, theories are constructed and again tested to account for the laws.

According to the modern philosophy of science, these things cannot be set in chronological order. It may sound sensible to collect facts before propounding theories. But this is not always wise, or even possible. People may sometimes need some kind of theory before they can decide what facts to collect or how to measure them. But *historically* the beginnings of science do seem to arise in something like the order I have given—simply because the earlier items are apparently less complicated than the later items.

Thus science usually begins with attempts to measure. And in bygone times the would-be scientist in a given field was often badly received precisely because of his attempts to submit esoteric beliefs to measurement. He was told that it would be impossible, or immoral, or blasphemous, or dangerous in some other way, to attempt any such thing. People felt strongly about this question, and often disposed of the innovating scientist by the ultimate form of censorship. So it was with management too. The earliest attempts to intervene in a process regarded as one of acumen and flair by so earthbound a procedure as measuring facts was rejected with derision. But this phase in the process is certainly over. Managers today are very much aware that they need data of every conceivable kind with which to manage. The innovation of measurement in management has taken most of this century so far to complete. Two most potent management aids have emerged from the battle that has now been won. The first is management accounting, which must be sharply distinguished from the long-standing activity of computing profit and loss, which was the job of the old Exchequer. Management accounting investigates every aspect of profit and loss in fine detail, distinguishing between the cost of a product and its value, distinguishing between money earned and cash flowing, and so on.

The second aid is work study. Although this could now be regarded as a routine technique of good management, its introduction was the beginning of management science. For men who set out to measure what actually happened in terms of time and materials when a job was done were substituting facts for beliefs. To this day, a manager who commissions a study of method or a study of time and motion on an operation that has not been studied before may expect to receive many surprises.

Figures Are Not Enough

Most of us are old enough to remember what fun everyone had about fifteen years ago with the joke: " I have made up my mind, don't confuse me with the facts." This joke, apart from being hoary, simply is not funny today. The need for facts and measurements is too well recognized. Yet this is only the beginning; unfortunately, all too many managers believe that the process of introducing science into their job is already complete. In industry, if an argument is supported by basic costings, it may be regarded as unassailable. When a government-sponsored report contains tables and graphs and statistical appendixes, it is hailed as scientific. But such marshaling of facts is really only the beginnings of a scientific process.

One of the first attempts to rationalize management was time-and-motion study. The illustration shows the movements involved in pulling a tankard of beer, as recorded in the time-and-motion-study engineers' shorthand. The first symbol (1) stands for "locate," the second (2) for "select," (3) "grasp," (4) "carry," (5) "move hand empty," (6) "move hand full," (7) "position," (8) "operate," (9) "inspect," (10) "move hand full," (11) "release," (12) "move hand empty."

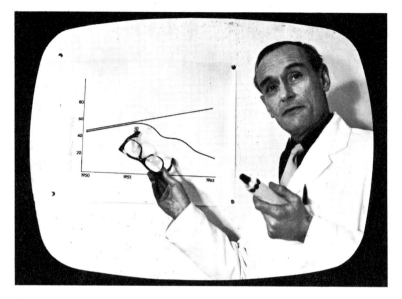

The prestige of present-day science is being put to many essentially non-scientific uses.

We ought, in fact, to be careful about degradation of the word " science." It has become seriously devalued. On the one hand, thanks to nuclear bombs and space research, the potency of science has been brought home to the ordinary run of people. On the other hand, the world of high-pressure selling exploits this new and powerful reputation of science to obtain endorsement for its products. Thus we wash our hair scientifically, clean our teeth with scientific toothpaste, and buy anything that bears the magic label " a miracle of modern science." The notion of what science really is, and the understanding of what scientists actually do, has been perverted.

The fact is that we cannot afford to use up our understanding of what science is about in this trivial fashion. For although science starts practically with observation and the recording of data, it is basically concerned with finding patterns of facts; and in particular with finding patterns that reproduce themselves. For it is in the understanding of such patterns that we achieve the capacity to do that one thing that distinguishes us men from the rest of the animals: to predict. It is this basic human capability, developed in a

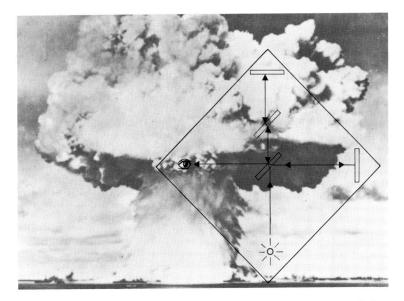

The facts on which the relativity theory is based were known long before Einstein's interpretation suggested unsuspected phenomena.

special context, that makes for the efficiency of the good manager.

The manager sees pattern in the behavior of the business, or that part of it for which he is responsible, as a whole. He will often say to an accountant: " You have given me data, and no doubt these data are true; but this is not just a question of cost—I have to consider the effect on customer goodwill, on labor relations, and many other things." So if management science is to be a reality, it has to go on devising and taking measures of things that may well be regarded as imponderable at this moment. It is not enough to sit back and admire the fact that certain, by now conventional, measurements have been taken and are made readily available. In particular, it is not enough to content ourselves with measurements of *processes*. The patterns in management activity that are really important are not concerned with processes, except insofar as these give content to ideas. The important patterns are concerned, as we said at the start, with policies and decisions and controls.

We have come to the critical point. Management science deploys a skill and methodology originally developed for the investigation of nature at large to do research into the manager's own job. It is

only trivially concerned with the processes being managed. It operates in an area dominated by hunch and value judgment; it sets out to determine what factors actually do influence affairs, and to measure those. Management science must also seek to incorporate the resulting quantities in some account of the situation, which includes hypotheses about the reasons for its working as it does, and the " laws " by which the whole situation is sustained. All this is going to involve more than measuring things; it is going to involve *operational research*. And again we must note that research into costs and processes will not be enough.

The Beginnings of Operational Research

Leading firms had traveled thus far in the years between the two World Wars. It took the second of these wars to carry the process of creating a management science one step further. The steps came about in the following way. Managers of war, which is to say generals and their counterparts in other services, are at a peculiar disadvantage from a purely management standpoint. This disadvantage is that their real knowledge and experience, the stuff that really counts, is acquired only in war itself. In peacetime they may contemplate war, analyze its past lessons, and plan for the future. But the process of gaining managerial knowledge and experience is at the least much retarded during peace. There was a very rapid development in science and technology immediately before World War II; but it was not fully assimilated into military thinking by

Opposite: Too close a view may interfere with one's grasp of an overall problem or concept.

War games are used to provide managerial experience for generals in the absence of wars. Management " games," in which managers make decisions about a " business " have become an important tool in management training.

any of the belligerents when World War II broke out. Each belligerent country discovered that its strategies had been overtaken by technological events and scientific opportunities that it had failed to evaluate properly.

Let us look at a few examples. The French army discovered it could not hold its country's boundaries by the use of that impregnable fortress the Maginot Line because there were new ways of circumventing such a stockade. The British discovered that their belief in invincible sea power was a delusion, and were nearly blockaded into defeat, because new methods of attack had been perfected but not predicted. The German air force found that its bombing strategies would not always bring their expected reward, because radar had been invented in the meantime. Apparently there was no lack of knowledge and experience anywhere; nor were the mighty arms of the nations deployed in 1939 without much measured data in support of the strategies and tactics employed. But the interactions of these new strategies had not been experienced and were not accurately predicted.

It is important to understand what was the matter. Superficially, one belligerent had simply not thought of a better weapon than the other: The problem appears to be the purely technical one of inventing an answer to this weapon, or of finding another still more effective. But there is much more to it than this. A land army organized for trench warfare is thrown into chaos by airborne landings because its defense strategy is inappropriate. It could have a different policy, and a more successful one, even while using its existing armory. By the same token, an industrial manager, an entrepreneur, or a government minister may command more or less efficient machines or other facilities than his competitor. But this is only one component of the battle. What counts is strategy, taking into account the possibilities open to the opposition.

It was in these wartime circumstances that the use of science to investigate strategy and tactics was developed by the British, under the title Operational Research (O.R.). The whole movement began with the development of radar in 1938. Here was a technological discovery that the scientists and the military quickly saw invalidated the air defense strategy of the United Kingdom. The strategy had been evolved on the understanding that the kind of information available in the event of war would suffer from limitations that radar transcended. Hence the military invited the scientists concerned to collaborate with them in evolving new strategies. The exercise was so successful that by 1941 there were operational research (O.R.) groups in all three of the British armed forces.

Lessons From Early Experience

This hothouse acceleration of the development of management science was exceedingly important, and provided many lessons for future civil applications. In the very first place, it emphasized that management and science ought to collaborate intimately, each providing a species of understanding peculiar to itself. The O.R. scientist certainly did not share the military manager's knowledge and experience of war; equally, the commander's knowledge of science was usually slight. The further development of management science therefore occurred as a close liaison under external pressures.

At present, the two parties to this collaboration often appear to regard themselves as natural enemies—which is absurd. For today the scientist (his suspicion of management exacerbated by what he may regard as the manager's smug belief that he is bound to be right) often appears to be demanding that science should take over the managerial task. The manager, on the other hand, begins to see a threat to his own dominion in the shape of the scientist (whom he correctly regards as ignorant of his business). This is no way to

The " Battle of Britain " in World War II—was successful only because it could be directed, from moment to moment, from this central control headquarters near London. This was made possible by information gathering and communication techniques unknown a few years previously.

advance anything, either management or science. And if there is to be a management science worthy of the name, then each component force must play a full and sympathetically respectful part.

The second thing learned of wartime O.R. was that the scientist who tackles a managerial situation for the first time has no prior warning of the kind of science that will have to be employed. Now it is obvious that science itself, the systematic knowledge of the world that mankind has, cannot be locked up whole and entire in the brain of any one scientist. The insights and the technical skills of many kinds of scientist may be required if an O.R. team is to make full use of science. Hence, in the early wartime O.R. groups, a mixture of scientists was to be found. They covered *between* them the whole range of scientific knowledge: O.R. became at once, and remains to this day, an interdisciplinary activity.

Another of the lessons that was quickly learned, and that has also been largely lost to view, was a rather subtle point about this question of measuring facts. If one wishes to devise a strategy for winning a battle by the use of science, it is no use waiting until all the relevant facts are known and have been recorded. The enemy is notoriously uncooperative about this. We may consider a conflict situation (whether military, or industrial, or commercial) as a game in which two sides are competing or at least in which one side competes with the vicissitudes of nature. Some such games—for instance, chess—are " games of complete information ": These are susceptible to *analysis* by the formal techniques of science. Most notably, it is a task for the applied mathematician to determine the nature of such a game, and the right strategy to use in a given circumstance.

But management deals essentially (not just by accident) in games of incomplete information, such as wars or the typical situation encountered in government, industry, and business. In a game of incomplete information, it is always possible to acquire *some* of the relevant information quite easily, and to acquire yet more by real ingenuity in the practice of empirical science. Later on, however, one encounters the real obstacles—and we reach a zone in which information is to be acquired only at great cost. In the military sphere, this is the realm of espionage; in civil life, it is the realm of very expensive research—whether technological, natural (such as geological, biological, or meteorological), or market. For practical reasons, in every important case there is likely to remain an area of total obscurity: Information about the game is never completed. Thus it is that O.R., as all empirical science, deals less in analysis and deduction, and more in experiment and induction. Given *all* the facts, a certain answer can be deduced; given only *some* of the facts, we have to find new ways of inferring a conclusion.

System, Prediction, and Profit
What then is O.R. trying to induce, to infer, by empirical methods? The answer is very clear. It is trying to discover the nature of the underlying system that generates the particular situation under study. If we know what that system is, how it is characterized by quantity, what are its logical relationships internally and with the rest of the world, then we acquire predictive power. And this is precisely the virtue of O.R.: A policy, a decision, a scheme of control, all these managerial commodities are successful insofar as they can cope with what will happen. It is not just a question of what happens now, it is a question of what is held in store. Although O.R. begins with the measurement of variables, it ends by computing in probabilities about future events.

It is worth highlighting in one story the difference between the present and the future, between deduction and induction, and between management based on the analysis of facts and management based on an understanding of the underlying system. The story is stupid, but the moral is sensible. An exercise often (and very properly) undertaken by accountants is to discover which parts of a business enterprise are the most profitable. It is then open to management to consider ways of improving the unprofitable parts, or to contemplate closing them down and extending the profitable parts. In a large department store, then, it was decided to find out which department had the highest turnover and return per square foot of floor space, and to see whether any conclusion could be drawn from the answer.

The costing (and here is the stage of the collection of basic data) revealed that the most profitable department was the Tea Room. There is a kind of managerial mind that supplied with this information, would conclude: We must turn the entire department store into a Restaurant. Observe that there is a spurious " now " in which this conclusion is correct: That is, if every customer now in the store could instantaneously be induced to take tea, the profits would exceed any ever made. But quite obviously this is impossible, and equally clearly the system that constitutes a department store will not permit the successful implementation of this policy in the future. For the new system created to maximize profit will not have any customers.

The conclusion drawn is not wrong just because it is ridiculous; there is a very definite reason for the mistake. It is this. In changing the character of a system that has generated a profit in Part A, we alter the expectation of profit in Part A. Therefore a policy for change that is based on a superficial analysis of the present situation, and the extrapolation of the results into a future that will have been made different by that very change, is probably wrong. We shall possibly find to our disgust that the new system does not generate a profit in Part A at all. This is surely the reason why so many grandiose development plans undertaken by industry do not make the return on capital that was forecast. The error is frequently met.

The answer is to use operational research to create a scientific account of the whole system that generates these profits. Such research will show what changes in that system would lead to a more profitable set of answers in the changed circumstances. It is clear that this can be done only within the context of the entire operation, and not by contemplating little bits of it. In short, the main facility offered to management by operational research is a capacity to visualize the enterprise as an organic whole, to determine the structure of the underlying system that makes it what it is, and to compute in terms of the dynamics of that system.

Understand First, Diagnose Second, Prescribe Third

As we shall discover later in this book, a quarter of a century of operational research practice in every field of management has resulted in a whole armory of special techniques, mainly mathematical, by which the value of alternative managerial policies can be effectively computed. These techniques are concerned to produce the best combination of factors in the search for higher profits. Because of their elegance for the scientist and their success rate for the manager, these techniques are often written about as if they constituted management science. But although these techniques are used by O.R. men, they are not what is central to the subject. The vital activity is the investigation of system: What makes things tick? This has to be investigated by empirical research. We have to understand; we have to quantify; we have to infer from incomplete information. Only when all this has been achieved (we shall see how later) can the computational techniques be employed.

This warning about confusing particular solutions to stereotyped problems with a proper understanding of management science seems very necessary today. No one would confuse the pharmaceutical chemist's dispensing of a prescription with the practice of medicine. Yet there is today a widespread attempt in many industrial companies, and to some extent in government, to make use of the powerful tools of the O.R. trade without undertaking the empirical science on which their application should alone be based. This is like copying out the prescription that did Mrs. Smith so much good, and hopefully applying it to oneself.

Let us try to sum up these preliminary thoughts. The origins of a scientific approach to management were concerned with the measurement of processes. This was a good start: It gave us management accounting and work study. But the intention to measure things does not exhaust the scientific method, nor does a concern for the processes it commands exhaust the management's role.

Managers are concerned with three intellectual tasks: policy-making, decision-taking, and control. Science can help with all three by investigating the real-life systems with which the manager deals. It finds out what makes them tick, quantifies the variables involved (whether it is already known how to do this or not), and sets about the job of prediction. What will this system do if managed in alternative ways? The comparison of the effectiveness of alternative courses of action is the job of operational research (O.R.).

We saw that O.R. sprang from wartime needs, and the circumstances teach us three major lessons. First, management problems concern situations about which information is essentially incomplete. We have to assess the cost of obtaining more information, and to propose ways (not yet described) of wringing the maximum understanding out of the minimum data. Second, since no one knows which branches of science will prove to be useful in attacking a particular problem, an O.R. team must represent as many scientific disciplines as possible.

The third lesson is the most important. The strategies that managers employ are at least as important as the facilities at their disposal. These strategies are ways of exploiting the entire system within the manager's command, taking account of what possibilities lie ahead, as a whole. This approach is contrasted with the orthodox analytic approach, whereby the system is examined piecemeal. Small advances made in particular localities of the system may actually turn out to be inimical to the health and success of the whole. The example of the fundamental change produced in the entire strategy of air defense by the technological innovation of radar was used. We shall discuss in Chapter 6 why there should be an equivalently fundamental change in management strategy as a result of the technological innovation of the electronic computer.

It is all very well to think about existing ways of doing things,

The complexity of a single business organization (Imperial Chemical Industries Ltd.) is shown in the proportion of income from each type of product (below, left): The map (key below, right) shows the proportion from each geographical market. Sales in 1964 were £720,200,000, and 120,000 employees made 12,000 products.

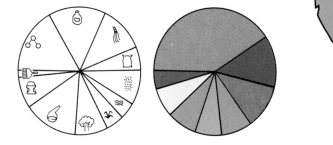

and to improve them systematically. But today we need to think again about the basic structures of management, and the overall problems that it faces. The main reason this looks so difficult is that the systems involved are so big. We do not really understand them, we cannot quantify them, and certainly our brains cannot undertake the necessary computations. Science stands ready to help with all this, and to use its modern techniques and tools in the manager's service. But we must not confuse the means with the end itself. The task is to solve problems, not to display clever scientific devices.

The very next point, which follows from this restatement of intention, is that time is a major constraint for management science. The manager who has a problem may have to give a decision by Thursday. It is not helpful, then, for the scientist to ask for three years in which to find the right answer. There are no " right answers," anyway: There are better or worse answers. If, by Thursday, the scientist can at all narrow the area of uncertainty that surrounds the decision, he has been of service. Of course, if more time is available, he can narrow that area further. But it is idle to plead scientific integrity in refusing to abide by the

manager's time-scale. It is also silly, for it suggests that scientists do not operate under any limitation at all. In fact, they are as stupid as most people, and they can do only what their current insight into the universe enables them to do. So shortage of time is just another limitation that the management scientist has to learn to accept.

This book tries to show how all this may be done. But there is a final point for contemplation before we leap into Chapter 2. We have talked about the manager's problems. But what are they? He knows what his *difficulties* are, assuredly; he lives with those all the time. But the problems that need solving are rather a different matter: They are the underlying things of which difficulties are mere symptoms. One of the things we have to do is to uncover what the real problems are, and these are locked up in the nature of the system that generates them. It is hard even to put a name to these real problems; and in naming them we often say less than it is comforting to think.

A man approached a boy with a dog. " Hallo, my boy," he said: " and what is your dog's name ?" The boy looked thoughtful. After a pause he replied: " I don't know. We call him Rover."

2 Chance, Risk and Malice

So we want to introduce measurement into strategic problems. We want to *compute* the answers to questions bearing on policy-making, decision-taking, and control. Some of the measurement, we said, is already there: We know how many factories we have, how many products, the sizes of things, and quite a lot about costs and processes. But the object is to invent a calculus of decision, and this has to take account from the outset of a further *kind* of natural quantity: chance.

It will probably help to take some time off at this point to understand quite clearly the basis on which this may be done. For there seems to be an extraordinary misapprehension among many people. It is this. Science seems to them to be about matters that are invariably determined. They think of the scientist as a coldly calculating brain that advances step by step from one fact to the next, uncovering the machinery of nature as it goes. And this machinery is like an engineer's machine, they feel, full of cogs and levers, specific effects following specific causes. Underlying it all at

Random deviations from a preferred position. The densest line of lights around the curve shows the line through the curve followed by the largest number of cars. Tracks deviating from this "preferred line" are presumably due to random differences in cars and drivers.

a submicroscopic level, they believe, are the molecules, atoms, and electrons, hurtling about like billiard balls, cannoning into each other and " half-balling " the red and the white for six points. I infer that they think thus, because they are prone to say that the world of business is quite unlike the world of science. When asked why, they say that the world of affairs is founded on chance, and all its decisions are risk-bearing.

Yet if these people would pause to reflect, they would realize that this mechanistic and deterministic view of nature is not held by science at all. The scientist's outlook in the 19th century was a little bit like this, perhaps; but a revolution started in about 1900 that quite changed the picture. It began in physics. Although one could say by classical theory what would happen when a gas was heated or pressurized, it was impossible to say what would happen to a particular molecule. Even schoolboys knew that gas volumes are related inversely to gas pressures—by Boyle's Law. But the fine structure of activity inside the gas was indescribable in terms of specific molecular interactions. Methods had to be found by which to describe the *chances* of those interactions instead.

Unpredictability, which is to say chance, had worked itself into science in a big way. Eventually Heisenberg showed that if you obtained full knowledge about the momentum of an electron, then it would be *impossible* to obtain full knowledge about its position. The universe, mankind discovered, is founded not only on unpredictability, but on a deep-seated uncertainty that cannot even in theory be resolved. Soon similar notions were turning up in other branches of science: in chemistry and genetics, in biology and psychology. By now the most important aspect of measurement in science might best be described as a business of evaluating chance in natural systems. The mathematical apparatus that goes with modern science is therefore especially designed to compute with probabilities rather than with certainties. And the scientist, like the businessman, sees his universe not so much as a collection of definite things but as a flux of uncertain interactions.

Getting to Grips with Chance
When I said at the end of the first paragraph that chance is a natural quantity, I meant it very literally. The odd thing is that

The orderly operation of chance is seen in many natural phenomena. It is predictable that a small fraction of the ears of wheat from a particular planting will be at least as large as the larger ear above; and that a small fraction will be at least as small as the smaller ear, the rest falling in between. Which ear will be which size is not predictable, however.

intelligent well-read people do know all this—and yet they bring into board rooms the archaic notion of deterministic science. It is a puzzle why this should be so. Perhaps it means that the sort of thing taught in schools is fifty years behind the sort of thing that scientists are actually doing. Thus we may carry over into the board room notions ingrained in us as children, and set aside the modern insights obtained from more recent reading. Perhaps—and this is more sinister—we unconsciously resent potential scientific interference with managerial prerogatives. But this should not be so.

Not only ought there to be an intimate collaboration between manager and scientist, but the manager himself—on his own—should be able to grapple with the idea of quantified chance. It is not that he ought to do the mathematics involved; he ought to know what mathematics to ask for. Meanwhile, in the absence of enough understanding to do so, we find him tricking out his speech so that value judgments are made to sound more rational than they really are. It was remarked in the last chapter that people will refer to any study as " scientific " if it has a few figures in it; perhaps this is comforting. But the device reaches the proportions of a swindle when we hear people speaking of " a calculated risk." What they really mean is that the risk is the one aspect of the problem that they *cannot* calculate.

Subjective guesses at probabilities are seldom very accurate, except in the simplest cases. For example, suppose 90 people are present in a room. What is the probability that at least two of the people present share the same birthday (same day and month, that is)? Some people divide 90 into 365 and say there is one chance in four (P=·25), which is a very bad guess. Others think the probability is much less. In this particular case, it can be shown that the probability is, in fact, P=·99998. Since P=1·0000 represents certainty, the chance of finding at least one pair of " birthday twins " in 90 people is as certain as anything is ever likely to be in this life. The mathematical analysis shows that the probability passes ·5 or 50 per cent (even odds) with only 23 people present.

The exact probability of finding at least one set of birthday twins in a group of r people is given by the formula:

$$P = 1 - \left[\left(1 - \tfrac{1}{365}\right)\left(1 - \tfrac{2}{365}\right)\left(1 - \tfrac{3}{365}\right)\cdots\left(1 - \tfrac{r-1}{365}\right)\right]$$

which will be tedious to calculate if r is large. Fortunately the mathematicians can show that the *approximation* formula

$$\log_e (1-P) = - \frac{r(r-1)}{2\,(365)}$$

gives results accurate for practical purposes.

The Use of Approximation
There are two points to make. Firstly, you will note that I italicized the word *approximation*. Because we have understood that

nature is uncertain, we must also acknowledge that it makes little sense to quote very precise figures in a situation that is itself not very precise. We should not have said 99·998 per cent, but 100 per cent. Yet people who are trying to be realists, and trying to use measurements, will often quote a figure such as £23,786,437. This figure may well have been obtained by adding up lots of little figures, each of which is supposed to be correct; therefore the total is supposed to be correct. But *supposed* is the operative word. The scientist knows that it is not possible to obtain measurements of this alleged accuracy, and he will try to stop the manager from using them. Again, if we are trying to choose between two courses, one of which (on scientific analysis) turns out to be very profitable and the other of which turns out to be disastrous, there is little point in carrying the quantification much further than a plus or minus sign.

The second point is this. In making the computation about birthdays, we made a *simplifying assumption*. It was that there is an equal chance that anyone is born on any day of the year. This, very probably, is not true: One can think of all sorts of reasons why birthdays may tend to cluster in particular parts of the year. In presenting this example to you, I could have insisted on setting this right; I could have set out to undertake empirical research into the way in which birthdays are actually distributed throughout the year. Would it not have been more scientific to do so? The answer, given in a vacuum, is yes. But I had to ask myself what I was trying to do with my example. It was, of course, to indicate that our subjective guesses at mathematical probabilities are often wildly in error. This I successfully did, without introducing the complication of clustering. If birthdays do indeed cluster, then the probability of finding two people with the same birthday will actually increase. If the effect of the simplifying assumption had been to *reduce* the odds, it would have been improper and unprofessional for me to have ignored the fact. But since the truth of the matter can only slightly increase the strength of my case, which is already quite good enough for the purpose in hand, there was no need to go to the " expense " of all this work.

Now these points about approximations and simplifying assumptions are matters that need great attention in business. We saw in

Chapter 1 how the beginnings of science in management have led managers to accept that facts are needed before decisions are taken. But this has been almost overaccepted. Tremendous expenses are incurred in overelaborate costing schemes, in undertaking market research uncritically into any and every aspect of demand, and in research and development work on features of the product that are irrelevant to sales. Thus if management science stops short at the idea of measuring things, it will lead (and indeed it has led) to waste. We shall have to see later how these pitfalls may be avoided. The job now is to return to the thread of the argument about chance.

How Simple is a Simple Situation?

The quantification of probabilities by algebraic analysis of the kind so far examined can be very useful. It is in essence exactly like saying: A die has six sides, and may fall on any one side; therefore, provided the die is unbiased, the probability of throwing a three is one-in-six, or a sixth. The probability of a pair of dice showing double three is multiplicative: The chance is now a thirty-sixth. But if we ask what is the most likely number to be thrown by a pair of

Probability calculations get rapidly complex when the same overall result can be obtained in several different ways. The diagrams above show why there is only one chance in 36 of getting a total of 12 points in a cast of two dice, while there are six chances out of 36 of getting a total of seven.

dice, the answer is not that all numbers have equal chances, but that 7 is the most likely. (Compare this with a process of the brain. If you ask enough people to give you a number at random between 1 and 12, most of them do say 7.) The whole business of quantifying probabilities becomes complicated rapidly, and the numbers soon become very big.

The most important practical use of combinatorial probability is in assessing the complexity of any situation that has to be controlled. When a manager is operating in the third of the roles in which he is cast, that of controller, it is vital that he achieves an understanding, if possible a quantified understanding, of the number of alternative combinations of events with which he has to deal. All too often, gross mistakes are made in setting up control systems by accepting a situation as it is at the moment. The result is that by next week, or next month, or next year, some of the factors have changed and the situation is not the situation that it was. The control system can no longer cope. But if we define the situation sufficiently clearly, then—because of these combinatorial proper-ties—we can measure the number of possible states it can take up.

These are the raw data we need to devise a workable control system. According to the science of cybernetics, which deals with the topic of control in every kind of system (mechanical, electronic, biological, human, economic, and so on), there is a natural law that governs the capacity of a control system to work. It says that the control must be capable of generating as much " variety " as the situation to be controlled. Now variety may be roughly defined as the possible number of distinguishable states in a situation. So the situation as we see it today is *one* pattern of a huge number of possible patterns, which is this measured variety.

Let us take an example. Suppose that there is a production unit housing ten processes. Incoming material is programmed onto some number of these ten processes (one kind of order needing only one process, another five, and so on). Moreover, we shall take the general case where the product may be sold at any stage. Currently, there is a typical pattern of orders and of sales that conditions the management to think in terms of a relatively few patterns of production. Thus if someone is asked to install a production control system in this place, he will almost certainly be

told (in a very familiar phrase) to put in something simple, cheap, and effective. The belief is that a simple control " cannot go wrong." The real question to ask is whether it can go right. For if we measure the variety of the situation just described, we may write down a formula to state the number of ways in which r processes may be chosen from the total n (in this case 10) processes for progressing incoming material and making a sale. The formula once again needs an awful lot of working out, and again we shall seek mathematical help in achieving an approximation that will give us roughly the right answer.
The formula is:

$$\text{Alternatives} = \sum_{r=1}^{n} \frac{n!}{(n-r)!}$$

and the approximation is: $\underline{A = en!}$

Now to the answer. There are nearly *ten million* possibilities, which the production manager of this tiny plant must control. Perhaps he is already using up quite a number of possible combinations, and a very large number of the possibilities may be technically infeasible. Even so, it is fairly evident that this simple little plant is vastly more complicated than it may appear. In particular, if responsibility falls on the manager to decide which set of patterns of production will be the most profitable, then he will have to do rather a lot of homework to exhaust the possible alternatives before reaching a conclusion. We shall see in the next chapter how the application of management science can help managers out of such a dilemma.

For the moment, the point is made. The potential uncertainty of real life is very much greater than the manager himself imagines, even though he may be busily explaining to the scientist how great it is. Any realization of a complicated situation in practice, then, has only one chance in millions of being as it is. We do not often think of things in this way. For example, if we sit down to play bridge and every one of the four participants is dealt a complete suit of cards, then we are truly amazed. We fail to realize that *every* hand dealt has an equivalently low chance of occurring.

In a sense, then, we ought to be continually amazed that things are as they are. Because we are not, we too readily accept the patterns that happen to exist, and fail to explore alternative patterns that might be much more profitable. We shall see more of this too in later chapters. The mental orientation that comes out of the argument so far is this: We normally regard a complicated situation as being built up of a lot of elements put together to form a vast and elaborate whole. By the use of a little imagination, however, we can just as well regard this same situation as being itself something very simple: just *one* choice out of millions of available choices. With this in mind, management becomes a task of chopping down possibilities to one actuality, rather than of building up small components to make an interacting whole.

How Near is Near Enough?

But despite our experience with dice, cards, and horses, and despite the relevance of probabilities regarded as realizations of one possibility from a number of alternatives, the most important aspect of chance in nature and in management is based on something other than combinatorial probability. This is the fact of variation. Nothing in the world is *exact*. That is to say, every measurement made of a natural quantity is accurate to some order of approximation. An acceptable degree of accuracy is determined by the use to which a measurement, or the thing measured, is to be put. Once this is admitted, then we also admit the idea of variation about some exact target of ours, a variation that is to occur within acceptable limits. If we are driving an automobile and stop for lunch, and the barmaid tells us that our destination is 100 miles farther on, we expect this measurement to be inaccurate by an acceptable amount. It would not cross the mind that she meant to give the right answer within 100 yards, but if she were 30 miles out we should raise an eyebrow. On the other hand a feeler gauge labeled 0·001 inches will not be 100 yards out of true, nor yet an inch, nor yet a thousandth of an inch. If it were, the next feeler gauge, labeled 0·002, would find itself in an ambiguous position.

So the idea of limits on accuracy is readily accommodated. The next step in the argument is this. If we are aiming at a certain notional exactitude, but will tolerate a discrepancy up to certain limits in both directions, then the following question has meaning. Is it *more likely* that we shall be nearer or farther away from the

40

A system with a small number of
parts can generate remarkable complexity. The diagram shows all the
different targets that can be formed
with rings of only four colors.

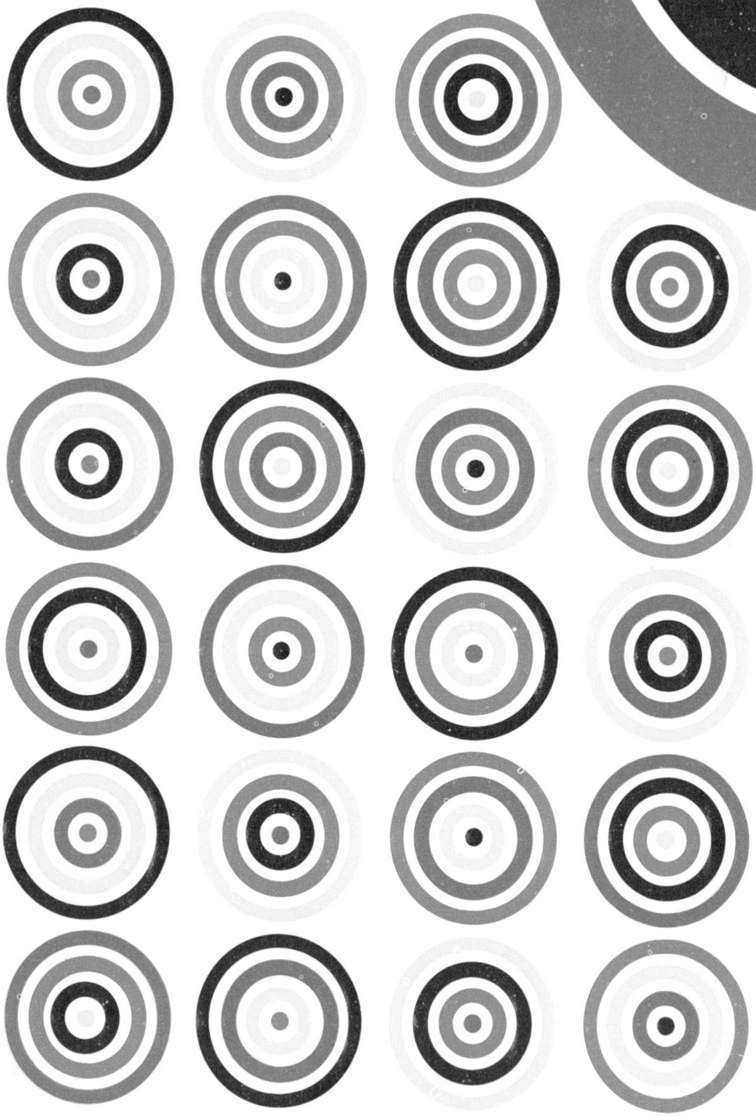

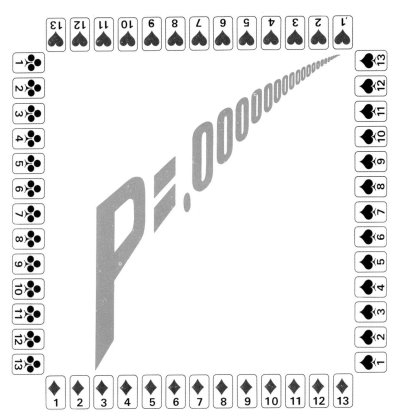

The probability of *any* specific hand at bridge is as low as the hand shown above. The probability is in fact a 2 preceded by a decimal point and 28 zeros ($P = 2 \times 10^{-29}$), if specification includes which player has which hand.

mark? It is in the concept of likelihood that a real understanding of probability resides, and we must learn how to measure it.

The Likelihood of Getting Near Enough

Imagine that in a bowling alley, instead of a set of ninepins (or in these days tenpins) there are, let us say, 11 channels facing us, labeled 0 to 10. This means that the channel labeled 5 is in the middle, and we are asked to bowl our balls into this channel. Clearly if our bowling is so bad that we miss the whole array at the

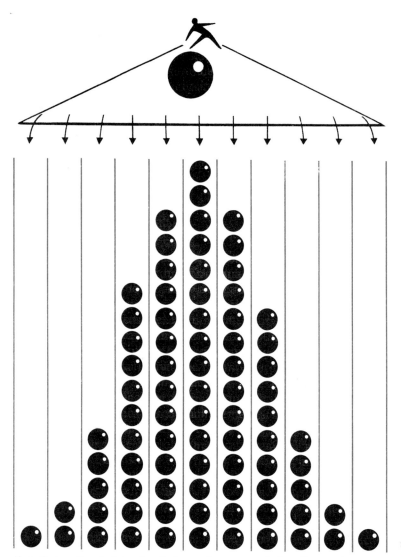

If each bowling ball is aimed down the center of the alley, and random disturbances are such that, on the average, one ball in 78 is far enough off to fall into the gutter on either side, the distribution of the balls, over the long run, will form the characteristic distribution shown above.

end of the alley, we have gone outside the acceptable limits. What is of interest is to know what will happen if we are good enough to get every ball into one channel or another. Given reasonable expertise, the bowler will get more balls into channel 5 than any of the others. But it is clear that his chance of entering either channel 4 or channel 6 is really rather high; he has only to miss 5 by a hairsbreadth to arrive in one or the other. There will be less risk of entering channel 3 or 7, and less still of entering 2 or 8. Occasionally things may go so wrong that the bowler reaches channel 1 or 9, and in the limit perhaps a very occasional ball may go into channel 0 or channel 10. If all the balls that are bowled accumulate in their channels on the floor, it is evident that a pattern will result something like that shown in the picture. At least, it will if the bowler shows no systematic bias to the left or to the right.

If this pattern were stood upright, so that the numbers were still along a base line and the balls were on top of one another, it would have a rather familiar bell-shaped appearance. The bell defines the compass of the events in which we are interested. The measure along the bottom shows a central value, which was the aim point labeled 5; and each step outward from this center shows a decreasing accuracy of aim in either direction. The vertical scale, measured out in balls, is in fact a measure of the *frequency* with which events occur. Thus most frequently the aim of 5 was met; less frequently but still very often the bowler was one unit off target; very infrequently he was five units away.

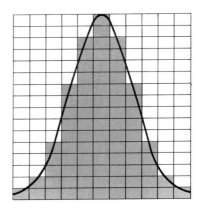

The idealized "natural shape of chance" or normal probability curve, as it is called, describes the actual variation of a number of phenomena quite accurately, although other types of distributions are also encountered.

This explanation of the frequency theory of probability seems to depend rather heavily on the flat euclidean dimensions of the bowling alley; but this is not really important. Let us expand the notion into a three-dimensional space, and imagine a dart player trying to hit a board. He throws several thousand darts, and we record the point at which every one lands. To miss the board altogether is to go outside the acceptable limits, and again we are interested only in the pattern of variation inside the board. Assuming that the player is really good, he will tend to hit the bull, or just miss the bull, with greatest frequency. Only occasionally will his darts land on the periphery of the board. A record showing the board with all the dart positions noted as tiny dots would consequently look very dark in the center and would fade away to a light scatter of pinpricks at the edges.

Now we could take the conventional wire grill off the dartboard and replace it with six concentric rings spaced at equal intervals. The middle ring would be the bull, and the remaining five annular spaces would indicate the five degrees by which the dart player failed to achieve the target. Placing this grill on the scorecard of hits provides us with a kind of contour map. The density of hits in each ring tells us what the " height " of the contour line is.

There was a splendid trick we learned in the geography class at school that always seemed nearly magical to me. It consisted in drawing a cross section of a piece of countryside by projection from a contour map. You doubtless remember how this is done. A ruler is placed across the contour map, and a mark is made wherever it crosses a contour line. These marks are then projected down onto a line representing a scale in miles, and a height is drawn to show the contour crossed at each point. Thus we can see the (somewhat distorted) shape of a cross-sectional cut through the actual terrain, appreciating the lie of the hills and valleys. If we repeat this trick with our dartboard, then the intervals at which the ruler cuts the contours will be equivalent, because the rings are concentric and equally spaced. In this way the base line of the projection to be made comes to be divided, as before, into eleven equal units. Next, we use the contour lines of dart-landing frequency to determine the heights. As can be seen, the result yields a " hill " of exactly the same shape as before.

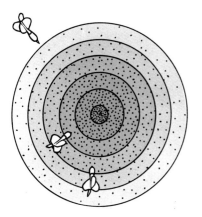

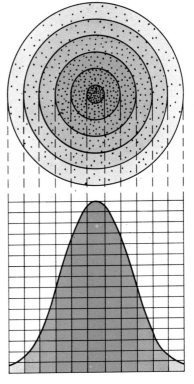

If the darts are aimed at the center of the dartboard, and the aim on each throw is disturbed by a collection of independent random errors, the results will generate a normal probability distribution as shown in the diagram at the right.

In fact, this is one of the great natural " shapes " of variation. It is so common in nature that it is often called the " normal curve." Often, also, it is called the Gaussian curve, after the very great mathematician, Gauss, who investigated its mathematical properties. Now the illustrations given are spatial, but normal variation is not really a spatial property. I have shown how it occurs in two dimensions and in three, and would be happy to go on to four or five or n dimensions if I knew how to illustrate them in a book. What matters is that all natural quantities tend to vary, and this variation has a shape dependent upon the frequencies with which individual events occur. And let us get an immediate and firm grasp

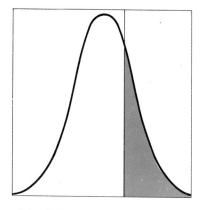

The area to the right of the vertical line, compared to the area under the complete curve, gives the proportion of cases falling in the area marked; in this case 27 per cent.

Opposite: Some variation in the output of any complex system is to be expected. The normal curve allows us to set reasonable limits within which we may ignore variations, attending only to variations falling outside those limits.

of the following point. Excellent predictions can be made about the shape of variation, although nothing (in most cases) can be said about the outcome of any one event.

How does all this lead to the measurement of probability? The last step of the argument is really very simple. For if, in a given example, a Gaussian curve is generated by a hundred events, and one of these events falls in the column marked " 10," then it is evident that the probability of scoring a ten is 1-in-100. But suppose that, out of a total of a hundred events, one typically has the value 10 (this being the tail end of the distribution), while two have the value 9, four have the value 8, and thirteen have the value 7 (we are approaching the dense center). Then it is also clear that the probability of an event having a value of *seven or more* is $1+2+4+13 = 20$ out of 100—or a chance of one fifth.

Thanks to the mathematical study of this curve, it is possible to assert the probability that a given event will fall between any two especially chosen limits. In fact, the chance that an event will occur *somewhere* within the " bell " is unity (that is, it is certain). Hence the probability that it will fall within any demarcated area under the curve is the fraction that that area constitutes of the whole.

Putting Probability Theory Into Action

This is the whole basis of the theory of probability. Most people in industry have seen it used in this quite primitive state in the form of statistical quality control. Typically, if a machine is producing

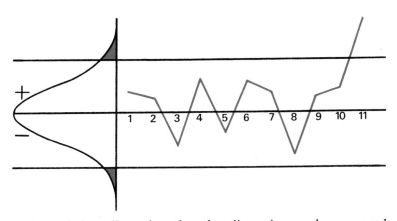

an item of given dimension, then that dimension can be measured in a large number of test samples, and the values are found to form a probability distribution. By setting acceptable limits on either side of the mean value, it is possible to detect when the machine needs resetting. Notice that these values are not chosen arbitrarily, but are fixed so that there is (say) one chance in twenty that they will be exceeded. In other words, the limits chop off the two tails of the distribution to just that point where 5 per cent of sample pieces may be expected to fall outside. As testing proceeds, it will soon become clear whether more than 5 per cent are so falling. When this happens, the machine is exceeding the chance expectation, and it is no longer sensible to believe that the machine setting is still correct. Therefore the machine is stopped and the setting reexamined.

For some extremely odd reason that I have never been able to fathom, this control technique is rarely used in any other industrial context than the one already mentioned. But I have used it myself to examine cost variances from standard, for instance, and it works very well.

Why should the manager be confronted with the variation from expected value in terms of the cost of every item that has passed through his department? The practice results in weekly cost returns several inches thick, which the manager has no time to examine. Perfectly ordinary accounting machinery (not to say computers) can be organized *not to print* the results they compute that lie within the expected variation about the mean. They will print only that (say) 5 per cent of cases that lie beyond these fiducial limits, as they are called. This means that the manager gets one page of cost returns for every twenty he used to get, and the only information that has been suppressed is statistically guaranteed to be of no interest.

Another point to notice forthwith is that these considerations, which apply so well to physical events, physical dimensions, and costs, apply also to *people*. A distribution of the ages of a random collection of people may be expected to conform to the Gaussian curve. Their heights will conform to such a curve too; so will their intelligence—if you can measure it. The accuracy with which people can do things, and other simple but important attributes of their behavior, will also turn out in the same way. This gives the first clue to the scientific handling of that notorious problem: the human element. People will always be found to say that, however far science progresses in the handling of physical and financial situations, the human situation is for ever beyond such treatment. This is rubbish. For the human being imports uncertainty into a situation just as any other kind of natural variable imports uncertainty, and the effects are no different. If a consignment of goods fails to arrive it does not matter much whether this is because a blizzard has forced the truck off the road, or because a clerk was stupid enough to send the goods to the wrong destination. In either case, the material is not there when it is wanted. In either case, the probability that it will not be there is measurable.

We have now encountered the reason why this chapter is headed *Chance, Risk, and Malice*. People often act maliciously; even more often they act in a way that appears malicious to someone who is trying to reach a goal—although their motives may in fact be pure. Equally, physical things themselves may seem to be ganging up on the unfortunate manager who is having a bad day; you have probably heard the phrase: " malice in the object." But our job is to deal with variation from whatever source it arrives. This is to be done by measuring it in terms of probability. Then this kind of measurement can be used along with the other familiar measurements to determine policy, to take decisions, and to institute controls.

Now this is not an elementary textbook on statistics, and we shall pursue the notion of probability distribution no further. To avoid any risk of misapprehension, however, it should be said that although the Gaussian distribution is a familiar one in nature and in management, it is by no means the only " shape of variation " that is encountered. There are many such shapes, and they are all interesting. Some of them are skewed to one side, some of them are flat, some of them are pointed, and one is even rectangular. Think, for example, of the frequency pattern that would be generated by a very large number of throws of an unbiased die. There would be six intervals on the bottom of the chart, and (in the long run) an exactly equal number of events in each column. The shaped distribution, on the contrary, may be imagined as resulting from the throws of a many-sided die that is heavily biased toward one result.

The people who know all this will by now be thoroughly bored. Those to whom it is quite new are most earnestly urged to read a non-mathematical book on statistics, which will fill out these notions for them in a fascinating way.

Assessing the Ideal Stock Size

The next step for us is to find out what use these measures of probability are in the management context. The first question asked is: What is a stock? It is a difficult question to answer, for all sorts of reasons. As a practical point, it may be noted that in industry and commerce, where all kinds of stocks are held, it is often the case that no one manager is responsible for determining their sizes. I have often thought that this is probably because no one has really answered the basic question just posed. Take Harry and Bill, for instance, who are managers of two departments in a works, the one feeding the other with raw material.

Harry is doing the supplying. He has a lot of confidence in his ability to feed Bill with what he needs from moment to moment—if only Bill had enough sense to give him a little advance notice of what he required. Bill, contends Harry, needs no stock of raw material at all; all he needs is to buck up his ideas and do a little prognosticating. Bill, who loves Harry like a brother, disputes this. He says that, however much notice he gives, Harry often fails to deliver the goods. He casts no aspersions on Harry's management ability, but for his part would feel happier if he had six months' supply of all possible materials in his own warehouse at all times. Along comes Joe, the finance man. He has noted the fluctuating stocks in Bill's warehouse, and suspects that an undue proportion of the company's capital investment is tied up therein. He talks with Bill, and asks why his stocks are so much larger than anyone else's. Bill tells his tale of woe, and Joe leaves convinced that it is time Harry was replaced. But wait until he hears Harry's story.

There are times when the observer of all these events feels that the actual stock levels in the warehouse have been derived as the resultant of the forces Bill, Harry, and Joe—measured in decibels. As a matter of amusement, I once set out to correlate the stock values held over a group of twelve departments with the awkwardness of the managers involved—as estimated in rank order by an independent colleague. The correlation was perfect. The way in which managements sometimes try to cope with this situation is by making a very careful classification of the kinds of stock that are needed by the enterprise. They distinguish between raw material and finished stocks, buffer stocks and inter-process stocks, warehouse stocks, depot stocks, and shelf stocks; and they sometimes add a few for good measure, such as strategic stocks. The point of this seems to be to settle responsibility for the investment involved —which of course is often very large. Then someone can be held responsible for assessing the " right " stock figure. But the whole process may end up in the pretense that all these stocks are fundamentally different from each other, whereas they are not.

Stock is quite simply, and always, a shock absorber between two interacting sets of probabilities. Consider two machines, A and B. A feeds B with material, which arrives from no other source. The average length of time taken to produce an item on machine A is (say) five hours. The average length of time to produce an item on machine B is also five hours. Splendid, say the commentators, this situation is nicely in balance. There is no need for a stock between the two machines. This conclusion is wrong; not just wrong, indeed, but (shall we say?) magnificently wrong.

As we have seen, the time taken to process an item on each of these machines will vary about the five-hour average. So the interaction is as shown in the picture. Take the lower arrow on the diagram. Machine A is having a tough time with its piece. The raw

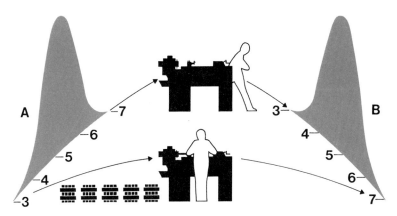

A convolution of probabilities. Machine A feeds parts to machine B for processing, and both machines have the same *average* processing time. However, if machine A is slow on a piece, machine B incurs idle time (negative stock). If machine A is relatively fast, a stock accumulates between A and B.

material is a bit faulty, the machine breaks a tool, there is something wrong with the lubrication, and the operator is pre-occupied with thoughts that his wife may run off with the lodger. Because of a concatenation of circumstances, then, the job takes not five hours but seven. There is a low probability that this will happen, but the probability exists. Simultaneously, and also by chance, the operator of machine *B* is having a splendid day. His material is easy-running, and so is his machine; he feels particularly fit, and has a date lined up for the evening. Because of this concatenation of circumstances, his piece goes through in three hours. (The likely discrepancies are exaggerated, of course, to explain the point more clearly.) Now the two probabilities are independent; there is no reason to think that the one affects the other—at least, not as told in our story, though in real life there may well be some interplay. If each of these events has a probability as low as 1-in-100, then the chance that they will happen *simultaneously* turns out to be 1-in-10,000. But it can still happen.

We now observe the result. Machine *B* will finish its work and will have to wait four hours for another job. There is a sort of vacuum in between the machines, which machine *A* cannot yet fill. This is why machine *B* needs a stock. To put the point the other way round, as indicated by the upper arrow in the diagram, machine *A* may have all the luck while machine *B* is unfortunate. In this case a piece will be waiting in front of machine *B* for four hours before it can be used. This is the thing that we call a stock. Therefore the stock between the two machines may be either positive or negative. But whichever it is, it certainly exists, and it varies between limits.

A little thought will now reveal why the conclusion that no stock is required was not only wrong but magnificently wrong. For the situation is asymmetrical. However long it takes machine *A* to finish an item, its operator can immediately begin on the next (a large stock for machine *A* is assumed). Machine *B*, on the other hand, can begin to work *only* if a piece awaits. Whenever the circumstance is reached that machine *B* has nothing to do, it incurs idle time. Hence if machine *B* sometimes incurs idle time whereas machine *A* never does, the stock in between the two machines will tend to go on growing for ever. I know that in practice the mess will be cleared up, but the principle is correct. If the two processes have the same average time and equivalent probability distributions, then the stock between becomes infinite.

It is really rather astonishing that people have often assumed in the past that a perfectly balanced situation of the kind described would be ideal, not spotting the terrible fallacy just explained. The point did not become really clear until mathematicians developed a method of analyzing the way in which two probability distributions randomly interact—this interaction being called a *convolution*. We can now see clearly that the size of a stock is a convolution of the input and output distributions, and that it has little to do with the beliefs of Bill, Harry, and Joe. So where does the manager come into the picture? The answer, again, is simple. The job of the manager in a stockholding situation is to say what probability he will accept of running out of stock—thereby incurring idle time on a machine, or stopping a whole department, or stopping a whole works, or failing to supply a customer who is asking for something out of stock. If the manager will just state this probability, the scientist will then be able to measure the probabilities involved and state what the stock size should be to meet the manager's need. This facility has a very important consequence. The probabilities governing the input to a stock and the output from it will vary with the item concerned. Any one manager may be responsible for thousands of such items, and the probabilities affecting them will vary. The convolutions of probabilities will vary too. But the manager's judgment as to the risk he is prepared to accept may not vary: He may treat this as an overriding policy matter. Therefore he has only to mention this one figure, and management science can set up the entire stock control system to take account of the individual variations of different items. Very likely a computer will be needed to do the job, but (contrary to popular superstition) it will probably pay for itself in no time. Notice also that there is no longer any need for office machinery simply to print out stock levels for the manager to inspect. It will compare the stock level as computed inside itself from day to day with the distribution of convolved probabilities worked out by the theory, *and will reorder*.

This means to say that the computer or other machinery installed to deal with this matter is actually taking a decision. You can say that it isn't, if you wish, and that it is simply applying rules that have been given to it, but take care—it may be that this was all the manager was doing anyway. For a managerial judgment of the sort we have been discussing probably involves as a subconscious act the computation of the probabilities we have now made explicit. When we said that a manager manages to manage by knowledge, we meant (to take this example) that he knew what the stock levels were, and how supply and demand were varying. When we said that he used experience to reach a judgment, we meant that the history of events, which is to say the frequencies involved, had registered in his brain.

It is better, I suggest, to accept that a stockholding decision *is* a decision, however it is taken, and to agree that—in this case—the way the trick is done has been exposed. Far from being a derogation of the manager, it is a signpost to freedom. If we can offload rather low-level decisions of this kind to machinery by the use of science, the manager is freed to attend to more important matters that have not been so laid bare.

Keeping the Queue to Acceptable Length

The mechanics of probability convolution as described are fundamental to almost any managerial activity operating in space and in time. The use of stockholding as an example was immaterial. Consider this: When things pile up between two points and we like what we see, we call the pile a stock; but when we dislike what we see, we call it a queue. Queues are stocks we should like to get rid of; and just as management is very concerned to keep its stock levels reasonably but not unduly high, so it may be a vital matter to try to eliminate queues without undue waste. The considerations involved are the same, and the science involved does not take us to any radically new thoughts.

If people are joining a queue at random for some service, then the intervals between the arrival of one person and the next are statistically distributed according to a well-known pattern. The shape of variation is not Gaussian, but we can still handle it. Again, we have no idea how long we shall have to wait before the next actual person joins; but we do know what the overall pattern will be. It is also possible, of course, to discover the distribution of service times: that is, the shape of the set of intervals between the service of one person and the next. Then we can compute the convolution of probabilities, and discuss the behavior of the queue.

This situation arises when people are queuing at a cash desk in a supermarket, for example. The fluctuating length of queue in front of the cash register can be examined as a convolution of the probability distribution according to which people arrive, and that according to which they are served. It is then possible to inform the management of the maximum length the queue is expected to reach. Obviously this will enable the manager to decide how many cash registers he requires to work, once he has taken the decision as to what risk he will run that customers may have to wait longer than a certain acceptable time. The answer will certainly vary on different days of the week, and at different times of the day. Consequently, a pattern of attendance at cash registers can be evolved, and a rota of salesgirls prepared to ensure that the right number of outlets from the store is manned at any time. In this way operational research will result in a more scientific and more efficient use of available manpower.

A typical queuing problem. The number of servicing stations could be increased, but the added expense might result in other aspects of the whole situation becoming unsatisfactory.

If this sounds an expensive sort of inquiry for a supermarket to indulge in, it must be noted that there is a strong likelihood that all supermarkets in a chain will demonstrate somewhat similar patterns of behavior. Therefore, if the job is done once, it can be administered throughout a hundred different stores. The same argument applies to appointment systems for doctors, hospital consultants, and other professional people. Simple rules have been evolved to ensure that the consultant runs little risk of wasting time, without his patients having to waste theirs by the hour. Perhaps the patients feel too ill to complain that these rules are not much used.

Sometimes the servicing of a queue is done in batches rather than as a continuous job. For example, a bus arrives, takes on a load of passengers, and goes away again. The mounting queue must then await the arrival of a second bus. This batching does not alter the fundamental science of the situation: It introduces a complication that the operational research man can readily handle. One gets the same effect with batch production in industry, in terms of the inter-process stocks involved, and in many other situations too.

Then take the question of how much stock to hold in a retail store. There is a queue of goods waiting to be sold, which we should more normally call a stock, uncoupling the retailing from the factory or depot. There is a queue of customers waiting to be served. The manager here has a host of problems, but all of them are amenable to the sort of theory we have been discussing. The volume and rate of sales determine the way in which the customer queue is served.

The results of this process, taken in conjunction with the arrival-of-goods distribution, determine the moment when stocks must be reordered. The frequency with which certain less popular sizes, colors, and styles are requested determines the need for such unpopular (in the manager's eyes) stockholding. It can all be worked out in terms of probabilities.

The strange thing is that once again it does not often seem to be done. Notice in particular that if any attempt is to be made to do jobs of this kind scientifically, then there will have to be some way of recording those customers' demands that cannot be met. Moreover, by the argument used before, the manager himself

The requirements of customers vary predictably also, frequently following the familiar normal curve. A policy of stocking or manufacturing only popular sizes of clothing will predictably lose a portion of the particular market.

needs this information if he is trying to make sensible judgments *without* the use of science. But how often is any provision made to collect this information? And what, I wonder, do *you* say when you have just demanded something in a shop only to be met by the reply: " There's no demand for it " ?

This kind of problem arises throughout industry, as well as in the retail trade. Very often, it emerges, management has taken a wrong decision. It tries to hold its most popular lines in stock, and treats less popular lines as the subject of special production. What happens then is this. A composite order is received calling for a selection of popular items and perhaps one unpopular item. Then the whole delivery is held up while the one extra is produced. This costs a lot of money, because the investment made in popular stocks is completely wasted, the extra item is produced under pressure and interferes with the production program, and the whole thing takes a lot of time and loses goodwill.

It often turns out that it would be more profitable in every way to reduce the popular stocks, and to hold at least minimal stocks of *all* items. But beware: Interesting conclusions like this, advanced from experience of particular cases, cannot be treated as generalizations.

The Genuinely Calculated Risk

These, then, are the bases on which scientists measure chance and risk, and incorporate some treatment of malice as well. Has it struck you yet that if automobile production in a factory is held up by a strike at the axle works, which may very well be malicious or pseudomalicious, that event may be described as a low-probability very-long-interval event in the distribution of arrivals? So what is all this talk about the human element? Either it will pay to hold a stock of axles or it will not. Whether it does depends on the convolution of the two probability distributions involved, including that very long interval in the far tail of the input distribution. Having created the distributions from actual records, this convolved probability can be computed, and the point put to the manager like this. " You must expect production to be stopped for between x and v length of time once in every z months. The loss to the company associated with such stoppages is between so-much and so-much per annum for x and for v respectively. By holding a stock of such-and-such a size, you will be able to keep production going on (say) half these occasions at a cost of so-much. By holding a stock of larger size, production will be secured nine times out of ten—or ninety-nine times out of a hundred (or whatever the manager wants to know). What are you going to do? " Here, then, is a manager being given a quantitative basis for a difficult decision: a good definition of what operational research tries to do. Here, at last, is the genuinely calculated risk.

A final point is this. We began our discussions of variability, frequency, and probability by talking about inaccurate *aim*. We were aiming at a target in the bowling alley and on the dartboard; management too is customarily aiming at some result. The Greek word for aim is *stochos*, and this is why mathematicians call the systems of convolutions between probability distributions that have been discussed in this chapter *stochastic processes*. There will be little attempt in this book to introduce technical jargon. But I suggest that this term " stochastic " is so useful that it ought to become part of the vocabulary of every manager. Remember that it involves aiming (we had better forget that *stochos* also means " guess "). A stochastic process is about the results of convolving probabilities—which is just what management is about, as well.

Low-probability events causing an unusual stoppage. A lorry delivering cars was involved in a road accident. The police charged the lorry driver and the delivery firm dismissed him. The remaining drivers struck in protest, over 20,000 cars accumulated, and the factory had to be closed for two weeks, at a cost, in lost production, of about $7,000,000.

A skewed probability distribution for delivery times. The left-hand tail is abbreviated, because deliveries cannot be made in less than no time; the right-hand tail is elongated, the probabilities represented being low, but not zero.

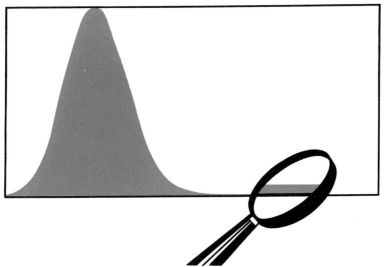

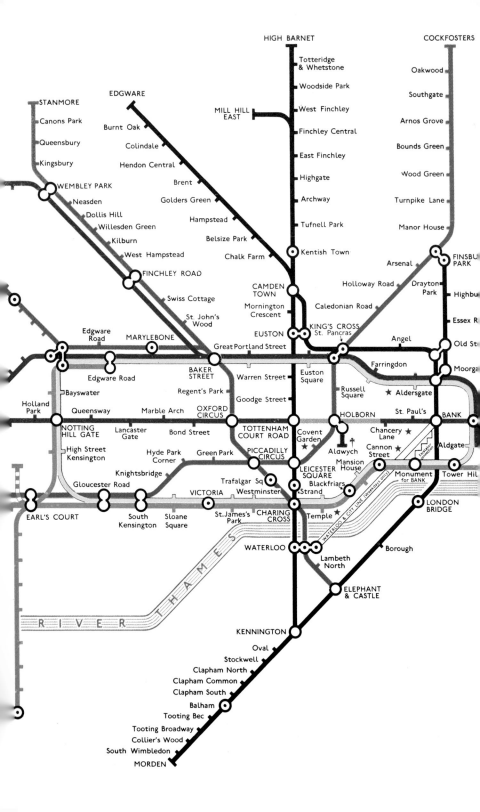

3 Quantified Insight

We have been talking about quantifying chance, and have thereby disclosed a rudimentary calculus of decision for risk-bearing situations. But although the kind of analysis we have been making will actually solve certain types of management problem, even some connected with policy, it will not in practice carry us very far on its own. This is because the management problem is normally more than a question of calculating risks. The aim of management science is to display the best course of action in a given set of circumstances, and this must include *all* the circumstances.

Although we have seen how to answer particular questions using particular techniques, we have not necessarily approached the ability to solve a problem. There is a difference. For example, the theory of queues might be used to " decide " that two more cashregistering outlets were required in that supermarket. But perhaps there is no space for another outlet; perhaps there is no staff to man it; perhaps there is no money to build the necessary equipment; perhaps—the list goes on. Certainly, one can think of

A model is valid for a particular purpose, if it allows valid conclusions to
be drawn. The London Underground
map (left), is valid for planning
routes to take between stations, but
is useless for determining accurate
distances between stations.

some queuing situations in which it cannot be even lightly assumed that people would prefer not to wait. Consider, for example, the doctor's waiting room, where there is some evidence that people go because they are lonely and want to consort with other people. Inventory theory may be used, as was seen, to answer all sorts of questions about the use of stocks. But if we put on blinkers and insist that a stock of some scarce raw material should be kept down to a given figure, we may wish that we hadn't when the stuff becomes unobtainable. To take a more normal case, it is not enough to solve the problem of stocks in terms of the decision calculus if there is a seasonal fluctuation in the price of the material being stocked.

Now a technician may apply techniques, if called upon to do so, and leave it to his employer to accept the consequences of having invited him to do what he has done. But the scientist is something more than a technician, and the management scientist is something more than an expert in out-of-the-way computations. He is committed, professionally, to the manager's service. Thus the answer " This is the best thing to do, and if you find you cannot do it then you will have to do something else, won't you? " does not count as a solution to a management problem. Hence the proviso that all the circumstances must be taken into account. Often, a manager does not disclose them; in that case it is the undoubted duty of the scientist to uncover them for himself.

This means to say that the scientist has to develop a method capable of containing all the aspects of the problem, although these will be of different kinds. Not everything can be expressed as a cost, or as a probability. How is he to set about the task?

The Situation and Its Models

Here we show a picture of one of those situations that the manager manages. It is not a very good picture. First of all, it exists in no more than two dimensions, whereas the managerial situation is multidimensional. Second, it has a clearly defined boundary, but the managerial situation is not so clearly split off from the rest of the world—that definite boundary line would more appropriately be drawn as a sort of fog. At least it has been possible to avoid picturing the situation as a neat rectangular box: No abstraction

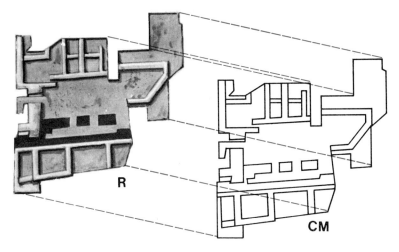

The conceptual model, CM, retains some features of the real situation, R, on the left, but is necessarily a simplification of the real system.

from real life is as beautifully simple as that. But the most serious shortcoming of the picture is that it does not at all convey the fact that the situation is generated by a very complicated system of men, materials, machinery, and money. These things, and the events that determine their states at any particular time, are supposed to be indicated by the dots. Remember that all of these are interacting.

Consider the manager who is confronted by this situation. He knows a lot about it; he has been there for some years, and before that he had experience of similar systems generating similar situations in his previous jobs. Here come knowledge and experience again. So in his mind is another kind of picture—his own understanding of the situation. This second picture is a much more accurate account of the situation than any that can be drawn on a piece of paper, but it is nonetheless defective. We are not provided with brains sufficiently big to take in and to comprehend with full awareness all the details of a real-life situation of any size. So the understanding that is in the manager's head may be thought of as some kind of *model* of the situation out there. His idea of the situation models the situation, and represents it.

This model is not a physical mock-up; indeed it is not visible to the eye at all. It is an idea. For this reason it is convenient to call it a *conceptual* model. This is the picture labeled CM in the diagram. The dotted line joining this model to the actual situation (with the picture of which we started) shows the manager fitting his notion of the facts onto the facts themselves. If the fit is very good, then he has an insight into the situation that is profound, and the decision he takes will inevitably be a good one; and vice versa. For, inevitably, bad and unprofitable decisions are the outcome of a misconception about the way the system actually works. As we said in Chapter 1, managerial activities are games of incomplete information.

The scientist calls the process of trying to fit the one picture onto the other, element by element, a *mapping*. It is a good word, although strictly speaking it is mathematical jargon. If nothing fits onto anything else, there is no mapping: Then this chap ought not to be a manager. He has got there by false pretenses, because he knows nothing more than the next man about what makes the situation tick. If the mapping were perfect, we should call the conceptual model *isomorphic* with reality. (This is a word from Greek, meaning " having the same form.")

An isomorphic model can be mapped onto the thing modeled element by element, one-to-one. Well, we have admitted the game of incomplete information, and the imperfect mapping. What actually happens is that whole complexes of things and events get registered in the model as single entities instead of complex ones. Thus the manager may think of a piece of plant (which is in reality made up of many subassemblies, each of which may go wrong separately, manned by different teams of men on three shifts) as simply " the Manchester plant." To this simple notion he will attach certain critical quantities, such as average outputs. He will tend to disregard variation about the average output, and its breakdown into kinds of product. Of course, just what simplifications of this sort a particular manager makes depends on his rank in management.

The sort of mapping that involves many-to-one transformations is no longer called isomorphic, but *homomorphic*. A good model is a homomorph, and we know the mathematical explanation of the

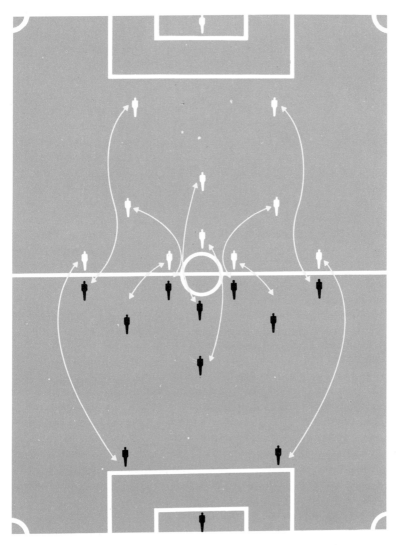

An isomorphic or 1 : 1 mapping of the strategy for the particular diagram above assigns a particular man on one team to attend to each man on the other team.

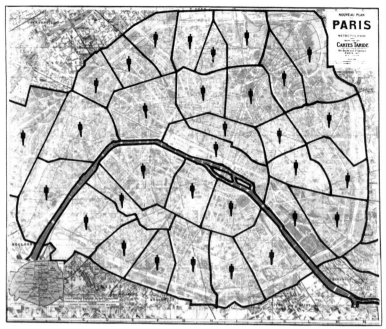

A representative legislature is a perfect example of a homomorphic or many-to-one mapping. The member for each of the electoral districts in the Paris area represents some tens of thousands of constituents.

way it works. Suffice it to say that a homomorphic mapping will preserve certain of the structural relationships in the thing modeled that are chosen to be preserved. And this is all that matters. For example, if the manager knows that the Manchester output is commonly greater than the Birmingham output, and suddenly one month he finds that it is less, he will be right to inquire why. (Incidentally, it may well be that all models are homomorphic rather than strictly isomorphic—except one. This is the model that reality constitutes of itself: a nice point for people of a philosophic turn of mind to contemplate.)

This, then, is an account of the manager at work, using a conceptual model derived from knowledge and experience of this and similar situations in the past. Consider next the state of mind of a scientist who is invited to examine this same situation. It is at once clear that, whatever his attitude is going to be, it must be quite unlike the manager's. For the operational research man knows nothing (except by accident) of the situation; he has not spent a lifetime in gaining knowledge and experience of it. He sees it for the first time. But if he is to work at all relevantly, then he too must develop a conceptual model. The question is, what kind of model? Just as, for a particular situation, the manager owns a storehouse of models that have accumulated from experience of similar situations in the past, so the scientist has a storehouse of models that may map onto that situation. The difference is that his models are derived from the knowledge and experience *of a scientist*. What has the scientific experience in common with the managerial experience? The answer is quite simply: system. The manager has an insight into this particular situation because of his experience of the very system that generated it. The scientist's insight comes from an experience of other systems in nature that turn out to behave in a similar way.

All this may sound like involving coincidence on a mammoth scale. But it is not. Nature itself, which is the scientist's realm of study, *is* a system; and situations handled by managers are very much part of nature. If there are laws of nature, then they are of universal applicability—provided that they have been correctly stated. Something dropped from a crane in a steelworks falls to the ground under exactly the same dispensation, and exactly the same quantitative rules, as the apple that is said to have dropped on Newton's head. The reason is that all physical systems are subject to pervasive gravitational forces. Any one of these systems can be mapped onto any other insofar as the falling process is concerned, *and the quantitative rules will apply*. As we know, this argument can be extended to rules quantified by probabilities too.

So the conceptual model entertained by the operational research man is a scientific analogy. It represents his understanding of the way that some natural systems work, and his perception that this is relevant to the managerial situation. Please note in passing that this distinction in the sort of conceptual model used firmly and finally disposes of the contention sometimes heard that operational research is a study undertaken by scientists because the manager has no time. In fact, it is an entirely different kind of activity.

The Scientist's Model
The scientific analogy as a conceptual model has also to fit the situation. Now a full-scale account of the theory of operational research would have to explain the mathematical sense in which

The last step in modeling a new industrial plant is the construction of a " pilot plant " essentially identical to the final plant except in scale.

this mapping is done. Unless there is such a sense, the analogy is a literary trick—not very scientific. It is no use simply stating an analogy, and just hoping that it is valid. But we may understand the principles of the answer to these difficulties by looking at the picture, labeled SM in the expanded diagram. SM stands for scientific model, a rigorous statement of the conceptual model (CM).

This business of rigor is critical: It is the point at which science has the edge on so many other serious and important ways of thinking, such as one finds in ethics or politics, for example. For science commands several formal languages that destroy ambiguity and equivocation. Briefly, to catalog them: There is mathematics, which deals rigorously with quantities; there is mathematical statistics, which deals rigorously with probabilities; and there is formal logic, which deals rigorously with qualities—in the sense of relationships connecting things. It is by setting down the model in rigorous terms that the scientist can determine the extent of its applicability to the situation. How far is the conceptual model, the analogy, valid? This is the question to which the scientific model supplies the answer. In the diagram, the

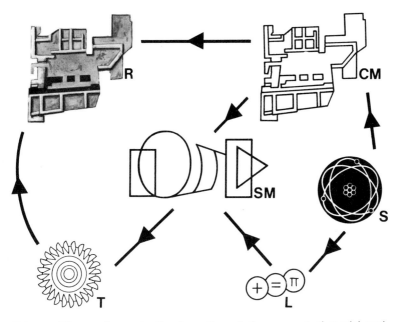

Science (S) contributes to the formation of the conceptual model and furnishes languages (L) that, together with the conceptual model, permit a scientific model (SM) of the real system to be formed. The scientific model furnishes techniques that permit the real situation (R), as well as the scientific model, to be manipulated.

conceptual model and the managerial situation alike are shown as mapping onto the scientific model.

Thus we are led to the complete diagram accounting for the way management science operates. Science itself, the box labeled S, supplies operational research with conceptual models, and with formal languages—the box labeled L. These languages are used in the creation of the rigorous scientific model (SM). From this model, which simultaneously represents both the managerial situation and the original conceptual insight into the system, the scientist derives his formalizations of technique. These appear in the box labeled T.

The model, it will be appreciated, has something in common with a hypothesis about the way the system works, and also with a theory about the rules that govern the situation. But it is something different in kind from both these traditional concepts. It is quite specifically a representation of the system with which the scientist can work. Especially, it is a rich and deep picture of that system. The idea is to account for all the factors that are involved, dealing with the difficulties presented in terms of homomorphic mappings, in order to discover what makes the system tick.

The manager knows inside him what makes the system tick, but he finds it hard to make this explicit or to quantify the insight. The scientist's job is to get at that underlying structure, to drag it into the light of day, and to quantify it. Now we saw in the last chapter some statements that would count as models of managerial situations—*if* the situations are correctly described in terms of (for instance) arrival distributions and service distributions. But, as was said a little earlier, this may not be all there is to it. If a situation is really more complicated, and relevantly more complicated, than a stochastic interaction reveals, then the model will have to be more comprehensive. In that case, the decision calculus already discussed cannot constitute the model itself; instead it becomes one of the techniques (in the box labeled T) for working on the scientific model and applying it to the real-life situation. In good management science practice this is what usually happens.

The scientific model is closely analogous to another form of quantified insight into the workings of a company. I refer to the balance sheet. This is assuredly a model of the firm, and is based on a homomorphic mapping—that is, there is a many-to-one transformation of events to entries in the balance sheet, which in turn attempts to preserve the basic structure of the situation by making the assets and liabilities balance. The notion " balance " belongs in common to the manager, and to the accountant, and to the scientist, since it is a very important quantifier of all their conceptual models. All natural systems must be in some kind of balance if they are to be in any sense stable and continuing. The scientist has various ways of discussing balance and stability, depending on what sort of scientist he is. The accountant who prepares the balance sheet has another way of expressing the same idea. But any one man's account is recorded in a single dimension, the dimension he understands. The balance sheet works as a model only insofar as aspects of the firm that can be expressed in financial terms are concerned. Equally, a statistician's decision model works in terms of chance. But a model from thermodynamics, for instance, would work in terms of entropy—which is another description of balance. In short, there is a rich profusion of models, of which the accountant's is only one, and the manager's another. The interdisciplinary operational research team ought to be able to provide a good many more.

The Balance Sheet, showing the financial position of the company, is a frequently used " model " of a business enterprise.

COMPANY BALANCE SHEET Imperial Chemical Industries Ltd

At 31st December 1964

Millions of £'s

NET ASSETS EMPLOYED			1963
Fixed Assets (Note 3) ..		441·0	419·7
Interests in Subsidiaries (Note 5)		226·0	134·1
Interests in Associated Companies (Note 6)		50·2	50·5
Courtaulds, Ltd Ordinary Stock (Note 1) ..			61·0
Net Current Assets			
Stocks at or under cost		69·6	61·5
Debtors		80·4	70·7
Marketable investments (Market value £27·2m.)		28·1	23·1
Short-term deposits		16·5	26·9
Cash ..		1·7	2·6
		196·3	184·8
Less:			
Creditors	56·7		37·3
Provisions for taxation and other liabilities	61·1		50·2
Bank overdrafts: unsec	1·6		5·1
	119·4		92·6
		76·9	92·2

The idea is that, in toying with conceptual models, the potentially most valuable may be selected as the basis for a scientific model to be expressed in rigorous terms. And what counts as the most valuable is not the " right " one amongst others that are " wrong." The most valuable is the one that most clearly reflects the qualities of the system that are most relevant to the problem situation. As a footnote, truth and falsity are attributes of statements about the world, and not attributes of the world itself. Insofar as we set up a model of the world in order to discuss it, then truth and falsity appertain to consistencies and inconsistencies in the model. So you will not expect the scientist to talk about the world itself as being true or false, but to refer to statements about it as being more or less useful. By the same token, the scientist hopes not to hear the accountant talk about " true costs " as if these were uniquely accurate statements about the manager's job. They are not. They are statements about the convention of accounting that have been used. If these conventions are good ones, then the answers are useful, but not true in the accepted sense of the word.

All this may explain why the manager so often finds himself unable to follow through the apparent consequences of a costing exercise. It very often happens that he will not act on an accounting conclusion that some particular bit of his empire does not pay. Almost equally often, he cannot really explain why he takes no notice. The answer is that his personal conceptual model of the total system concerned is more extensive, more ramified, and indeed richer in dimensions, than the accounting model that gives him the advice. The management scientist will try to model on this scale as well.

Meeting Deadlines in a Complex Operation
Let us now begin to make use of this newly discovered notion of models, by picking up the story of decision theory where we left it at the end of Chapter 2. You will remember that we talked about stocks and queues, and in general about those convolutions of probabilities called stochastic processes. So far we have considered only that very simple interaction in which there is one input and one output. This is all very well in the kind of problem that was then being considered. But the real problems of management are

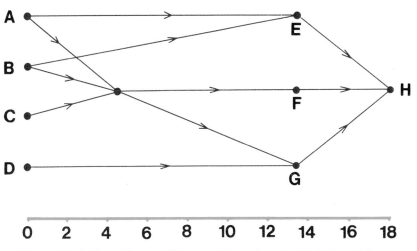

A very simple flow diagram. The event E requires that both A and B are complete; F requires that A, B, and C are complete; G requires that A, B, C, and D are all complete; and finally, H depends on the completion of E, F, and G. The horizontal scale is time, in days, for example.

often far more complicated than this. In particular, a situation under a manager's control is likely to be made up of a whole *network* of material flows, or transportation flows, or some other kinds of flow. A diagram of this looks like a madman's knitting, and not at all like the simple figure used when the discussion began.

Here is another picture, in which some flows are spread out in space and in time. Time is certainly an axis of the diagram—the horizontal one: Space is rather loosely represented in the vertical dimension. Wherever these flows converge, there is a nodal point, represented by one of the dots; and whenever a node in the network is reached, we are really concerned with a convolution of probabilities. This is what makes the manager's job so difficult. He may draw himself a diagram of this kind, or represent it on a planning board (some people will be familiar with the Gantt chart, which has much the same idea), but what is he to do next? The diagram, or the board, or the chart, looks as if everything will work out splendidly. But this is only because it portrays just that mechanistic and deterministic universe that we agreed long ago does not exist.

What we are dealing with here is a highly complicated stochastic process. It may be described as an interacting system of queues, or an interacting system of positive and negative stocks. Whether the network represents people queuing for buses, or customers queuing for goods, or materials queuing for machines, or capital queuing for investment, it makes no difference. I cannot offhand think of any sort of manager who would not recognize this picture as something to do with him—given the right set of labels. Let us begin to penetrate this particular mystery by taking an example. We will suppose that the network represents the flow of materials, and then manufactured items, and then subassemblies, and then assemblies, all of which are converging on a single and final node. This represents a completed job. It may be a house, or a ship, or a highway: It does not matter. The manager for whom this network is drawn is trying to control a building process that will result in a completed job by a specified date.

Clearly the manager cannot personally supervise every flow and every node in the network, if it is at all elaborate. He has under-managers, supervisors, and so forth, to look after bits of the total system. The question is this: What sort of control arrangements should he make to govern the whole thing? And if he has this considerable staff looking after the system, can he perhaps afford to go away on holiday? I shall try to answer both these questions.

The first point to note is that not all the lines in our picture are equally important. If you are building a house, it is evident that the electrical wiring can go in at almost any time after the shell is completed, so long as too much finishing (in particular, the decoration) has not been done. On the other hand, difficulties would arise if one attempted to put on the roof before the walls had been built. There is, then, a logical priority about the arrangements, and logic has nothing to do with time. Therefore, if it is logically necessary to do both A and B before C, and A happens to take much longer than B, then it is critical to the outcome that A be completed in the shortest possible time. B has more freedom, more slack, on its line toward completion.

Think this one over for a while. If we take any time interval, T1 to T2, out of the total network, we shall find that an awful lot of things are supposed to be happening in this period. Some of these

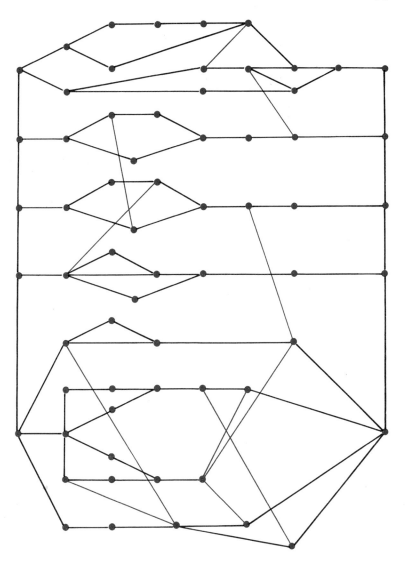

A more realistic flow diagram for a major project. Actually the diagram is only complex enough to represent the major aspects of the project; each major step would break down into similarly complex minor steps. Again, time flows from left to right.

will be relatively unimportant, in the sense that there is a great deal of time in which to do them. Others will be a bit tighter. And one will be the tightest of all. This is the one that the manager has to examine. If he can get this critical job done in the time allocated, then he is all right at time T2, and he can start to think about the next interval, from T2 to T3. This interval will also have a most critical activity within it. If we now stand back and review the whole system, it becomes evident that the maze affords only one pathway of which *all* the components are critical in this sense. The operational research scientist calls this the *critical path*.

Now any manager can advise himself that it would be a good idea to ensure that events that are supposed to occur on this critical path do occur on time. But he will have some difficulty, in a real-life example, in discovering what is the critical path. Here the operational research man can help him, because there are ways of computing the answer by a technique called *network analysis*. But more can be done than this. Each of the nodes on the critical path is really, as we said before, a convolution of probabilities. Using the calculus of decision, it will clearly be possible to nominate not only the expected times at which all these events should happen, and therefore the completion date for the whole job, but also the probabilities affecting natural variations about these expectations.

There are several ways of doing this, and the method actually used should be devised to suit the sort of problem in hand. The most famous of them is undoubtedly PERT, which stands for Program Evaluation and Review Technique, but it is against the author's management policy in the writing of this book to go into a lot of technical detail. The important thing to understand is that we can certainly get at measures of the best and worst total times involved in walking the critical path, according to certain probabilistic assumptions that the scientist will agree with the manager. Now we have a tool of control that depends upon the decision calculus, backed by a quantitative insight into the system that is generating all the problems.

Given this tool, the manager will be able to concentrate upon the jobs that matter most at any particular time, and to assess the effects of delays (and, if he is lucky, of unexpected time savings) on the entire operation. At all times, then, he will direct his forces in such a way as to dovetail their activities, thus ensuring that a conclusion is reached at the earliest possible moment.

Delay and Amplified Delay

Consider now the second of the questions posed earlier. Can the manager go on holiday, confident in the knowledge that he has delegated his powers to subordinates who between them exhaust responsibility for the whole system? The answer is emphatically no, for the good old-fashioned philosophic reason that the whole is greater than the sum of the parts. Let us see why this should be the case. Soon after we have set off along the critical path, there is a catastrophe of some kind. Let us say that we have been working on the assumption that the worst that can happen to us is that the time actually taken for one of the activities will exceed the expected time by a margin so wide that its chance of materializing is only one in a thousand. If this was the figure we agreed on, then to encounter this

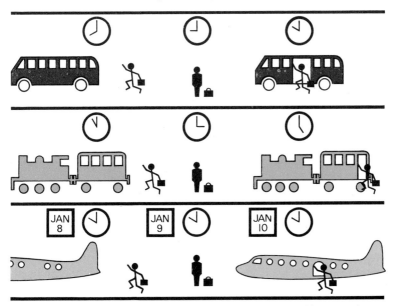

A three-stage delay amplifier. A traveler just misses a bus and has to wait two hours for the next causing him to just miss a train and incur a six-hour delay; this causes him to miss his airplane and incur a two-day delay.

unlikely event in real life is extremely bad luck. Not only does it happen infrequently (only once in a thousand times), but it also destroys the whole plan. For, by the manager's instruction, the play of chance within the network was devised to accommodate risks up to this order, but not greater risks. Well, the thing has happened. It seems to follow that we cannot possibly adhere to the original critical path. The situation now is that there is a *new* critical path—from the point we have reached to the end of the line. This has to be recomputed. In a really complicated network, this task of computing and recomputing critical paths means that an electronic computer has to be involved in management control.

But there is more to come. If this were all that mattered, the manager could well be on holiday. He could leave it to the scientist to recompute a critical path, and to inform everyone accordingly. The early job that caused the trouble was, let us say, a week late. This means that we can no longer guarantee to complete on time, but we still have a chance of doing so, because an unlikely probability may turn up in our favor later on. So long as we have recalculated the critical path and now adhere to it, we have done the best thing that it is possible to do. But the something more that matters is this: It is perfectly possible that a recalculated critical path will show that the job is delayed by, say, six months.

How can this happen? Return to the simple example of the building of a house. The woodwork is subcontracted to a firm of carpenters, and they have arranged to come in on Thursday. But something has gone wrong with the critical path control of digging the foundations and laying the first courses of bricks. We tell the carpenters that we are late, and that they must come not *this* Thursday but *next* Thursday. We all know what the carpenters are likely to say. Next Thursday they are due to put in the woodwork for a whole row of other houses. They will not be free until March. In this way a network can become an *amplifier* of delay. We may only just miss the bus; nonetheless we have to wait twenty minutes for the next. Obviously, someone using the tool of critical path analysis can compute the extent to which a delay may now be amplified by the end of the line.

A small delay, then, may be amplified to an excessive delay; moreover, there may be penalty clauses, and other expenses to consider.

Thus the subordinate manager who says he is sorry he is going to be a week late on his phase of the job, may all unknowingly be proposing to ruin your business. But the quantified insight of operational research will quickly show the cost involved. Now we may hazard a guess at the outcome. Suppose the trouble is a shortage of a particular kind of craftsman. "We have," says the subordinate manager, "drawn in everybody for miles around. They come in by specially chartered buses every day. There is *nothing* more we can do." "Don't you believe it," replies the manager. "These particular craftsmen, as I happen to know, are heavily under-employed in another country. We will charter a jet aircraft and bring them over."

It would be interesting to see the face of the subordinate manager who receives the decision. But the facts are clear enough. Within the compass of his own authority and responsibility, he has literally done all that he can. The kind of action now mooted to him appears, within his own context, absurd. But the manager may find a new solution transcending all the contextual limitations of his junior. This is why he must stay.

Models as Media for Simulation

Now this interlude has provided an extension of decision theory, to take us to elaborate stochastic processes rather than simple ones. It has also provided further illustrations of the use of management science. But this chapter is really about method, and I want to return to the discussion of models for a moment. The question is whether a probabilistically quantified network of the type discussed is or is not a scientific model in the sense already defined. Most operational research workers, I suspect, would say that it is. But my own answer is qualified. Just as a queue-theoretic account of a situation may be a suitable model thereof *if no other factors are present in the problem as it confronts the manager*, so may the critical path network constitute a model. But just as other factors than those measured by the decision calculus may impinge on the situation in the queuing or inventory study, so may other factors enter into the critical path problem.

If they do, the answer is the same as before. Decision theory does not offer an adequate scientific model: What it offers is a

"Sanders speaking. Stop all production on XP15, recall all shipments, wire
every doctor in the country, and hurry!"

The results of research and development efforts are, by definition, not always predictable.

technique for solving part of the problem—given that an adequate model of the whole problem can first be constructed. We have always to remember that we are talking about the system that underlies the managerial situation. Nothing counts as a scientific model of this system that leaves out a major share of the factors involved. But anything that will help to resolve even part of the problem may be accounted a relevant technique. The distinction is not pedantic, as we have already seen. Moreover, there is a very special reason, which we have not yet met, for demanding that models should be adequate accounts of the system-at-large.

We are talking about deploying the scientific method in the service of management. We have talked of the need for measurement, not only of the obvious physical quantities involved, but also of chance and risk. Next, we have talked about the importance of discovering what makes a system tick, and have carried the notion of quantification into the heart of the system by proposing the construction of models that reflect the deep interactions of all the factors concerned. There is another mark of science that has so far been overlooked. This is the notion of experiment.

The reason why scientists insist on experimenting is not as superficial as it seems. Quite obviously, and also quite validly, the scientist wants to explore the situation he is investigating, and experiment is a method of exploration. But the deeper reason why the scientist experiments is that he is trying to validate his model. He wants to know whether the model fits the situation in a dynamic and lasting way. Consider: A newly dead mouse is a very fine model of a live mouse in many ways. Anatomically and in all sorts of other respects it constitutes an isomorphic mapping. But you and I know that within a very short space of time this model will be denatured; in a week's time it will hardly be recognizable as a model at all. I apologize for being gruesome, but an example of this kind best illustrates the point. The situation the manager controls is essentially viable: It goes on living. The scientist faces a risk that he may map the situation more or less instantaneously onto some model that for the moment looks all right, but that may not develop through time in the way the situation develops. Even if it does, this may be a fluke. Experiment is a way of introducing specific changes into a model to see if it reacts as the situation is recorded as reacting to actual changes of the same kind. And in most spheres of scientific work this methodological requirement presents no special difficulty. The management scientist, however, is at once in great trouble.

The reason is that the management scientist is concerned with the same situation that concerns the manager. He is trying to advise on a policy matter. Inevitably, the experiments that occur to him involve fairly extensive changes in the real-life system. So he finds himself wanting to say to the manager: Let us pull down that factory, abandon all the television advertising, build a depot at the North Pole, and see what happens. From the point of view of scientific method, this sort of experiment could well be very valuable. But the scientist who proposes it to a manager will find himself locked up. In short, any series of experiments with a managerial situation that is likely to provide valuable information could be disastrous to the enterprise. We must go further. To be classical about scientific method, the scientist must deliberately take any proposed strategy experimentally to its limits, and explore the circumstances in which the firm is ruined.

So this is the main reason why the methodology of models is so central to management science. Given a model, this range of experiment, even to these limits, becomes immediately available to the scientist. *He experiments on the model instead of on the firm.* If the model of the company goes bankrupt, nobody cares—except the scientist. He is delighted, because he knows the limit of the effectiveness of the policy he has been studying.

This procedure is known as simulation. The model is to be used as a real-life surrogate. We may soon grasp what simulation actually involves by deciding how to simulate a straightforward stochastic interaction of the kind discussed in Chapter 2. We have a distribution of arrival times and a distribution of service times, and we want to know what kind of queue builds up between them. In so straightforward a situation, this can be done by mathematical means; but when it comes to a giant network of stochastic processes with huge numbers of interactions and feedbacks, the task is quite beyond the mathematician. It is then that simulation is needed, but the principle can be demonstrated in the simpler case.

Think for a moment about the distribution of arrival times. We remind ourselves that we know the pattern of variation in the long run, but have no inkling of the next event. All we know about that is the probability of its occurrence, which is implied by the measured distribution involved. Let us then divide that total distribution into a hundred equal squares. This will mean turning the smooth outline into a histogram having steps up one side and down the other, but no matter. On each of the squares we write the time interval designated by the column in which the square occurs. Hence the mode of the distribution (which is the tallest column) has the greatest number of squares all bearing the same figure indicated on the base line. Only one of the squares will bear the number on the extreme right or the extreme left, because the frequency of these values is so rare. Having done this, we take a pair of scissors and cut up the distribution into its small-square components. These we place in a hat, and shake them well. Exactly the same procedure is followed for the service distribution, the components of which are placed in a second hat. Simulation can now begin.

Taking a sheet of paper with the time-scale along the bottom, we start a fictitious log of the servicing process. Someone must arrive, and his arrival is marked down on the chart. Since he is all alone, it is possible to begin serving him at once. What we need to know now is how long the service will take. Dipping into the service-time hat, we withdraw a number. This is the simulated service time for this customer, and we mark his service on the time chart. The number goes back in the hat. But at a certain interval after the first man arrived, another is due to come. When? This is discovered by drawing a number from the arrival-times hat, and a second simulated arrival is plotted on the chart. Of course, the second man may arrive before the service of the first man is complete (I just do not know): If so, he at once begins to form a queue. On the other hand, the service may be over before the second man arrives, in which case the server is marked as idle for the intervening period.

This procedure imitates real life quite successfully. It will be noted that people arrive at random, as they really do, because the experimenter has no means of knowing which number will come out of the hat next. But because each number, when drawn, goes back into the hat, a sufficiently long experiment—say, for argument's sake, ten thousand draws—will clearly distribute the

If the diagram (right) were mounted on cardboard and the squares cut out and mixed in a hat, numbers drawn randomly from the hat would provide "randomly varying" data for a simulation experiment. To preserve the shape of the distribution, each number, when drawn, must be replaced before another number is drawn.

0	1	2	3	4	5	6	7	8	9	10
					5					
					5					
				4	5	6				
				4	5	6				
				4	5	6				
				4	5	6				
			3	4	5	6	7			
			3	4	5	6	7			
			3	4	5	6	7			
			3	4	5	6	7			
			3	4	5	6	7			
		2	3	4	5	6	7	8		
		2	3	4	5	6	7	8		
		2	3	4	5	6	7	8		
	1	2	3	4	5	6	7	8	9	
0	1	2	3	4	5	6	7	8	9	10

times used in a fashion quite typical of the real-life situation. It is clear that with sufficient patience one could use this method to simulate even the most complicated of systems. Indeed, when operational research first went into industry at the end of World War II, we did just this kind of thing. Very exhausting it was, too. Today, however, the scientist has the electronic computer as a tool. All he has to do is to store the probability distributions involved inside the machine, and to generate numbers at random that will instruct the machine which bits of the distribution to use. Again we have the facility that a genuine experiment is occurring: No one can say what the fictitious log will look like. But again it can be guaranteed that the overall pattern of variation will conform to reality. There is no need, moreover, to study the fictitious log: All we need is a print-out from the machine showing how the queue is fluctuating with time. In a complicated production simulation, we shall cause the machine to print out the amounts of idle time being incurred on each piece of plant. If the result looks unpleasing, then the stock levels can be altered, and the experiment run all over again to find out whether the idle time has disappeared. Indeed, a graph can be plotted to show how losses resulting from idle time are related to investments in stocks. And this is just the graph the manager needs as a quantitative basis for his decisions.

It will be realized that an immense amount of calculation will be required inside the computer as the experimenter really gets the bit between his teeth. For he will want to try out all sorts of possible stock levels, all sorts of arrangements for servicing, all sorts of investment plans. And as soon as the manager he is trying to help hears about this, he too will start to contribute a mass of ideas to be tested. Perhaps it all sounds rather overwhelming. First we must try to grasp just how fast the modern computer is.

Everyone " knows " that computers work very quickly, and we can turn to each other and say: Yes, they work in *nanoseconds* these days. We may even know what a nanosecond is—a millimicrosecond, which is 10^{-9} of a second. But although it sounds very knowledgeable to talk like this, it is really rather doubtful whether we understand what we are saying. It may help, then, to put the matter in this way. There are as many nanoseconds in one second as there are seconds in thirty years. This is how fast the computer is.

Small wonder, then, that if simulation starts after coffee, we know by lunchtime in just what circumstances the company might be bankrupt in twenty years' time.

The Payoff of Simulation

As was said before, the scientist is very happy with this approach because it enables him to experiment with a situation without doing any damage, and without waiting years and years to see whether he is right or not. The trick works with all kinds of model, and not just with stochastic networks. And indeed there are at least two vastly important uses for simulation other than the immediate and straightforward uses of identifying a correct decision, formulating a profitable policy, or devising a viable control. The first is to plan the implementation of any of these things in great detail.

When we know what it is we want to achieve, and even how to go about achieving it, we still have the task of phasing developments so that we can get from our present position to the intended position securely, sensibly, and economically. By setting up all the steps in the process on the simulated model and trying them all out under various conditions, the scientist can provide his manager with as near foolproof a plan as could exist. Moreover, it is possible to bring the managers who will be concerned with this development into the simulation themselves, in order to give them experience. To do this, one takes the management decision function out of the computer program and restores it to the managers.

This constitutes a new sort of procedure, which may be called a simulation game. The managers sit in a room with displays before them representing the state of affairs. The computer operates (very quickly, of course) until it needs a managerial decision. It then stops the clock, which is part of the display, and which has been whizzing round at many times normal speed, and sets up the new state of affairs on the display. There is a pause while the managers concerned assimilate this information, and then the appropriate manager—after normal consultation—takes a decision of which the computer is promptly informed. The computer can then rush its simulation forward until another decision is required, and so on. By these means it is possible to " experience " several weeks of management (in terms of these decisions, at any rate) every day.

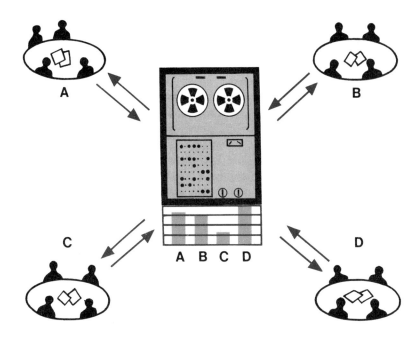

A competitive simulation situation. Four teams of " managers " operate competitive companies, trying market and production strategies, etc. The computer, furnished with a model of the complete industry and market, feeds back information to the " managers " and also keeps score.

The simulation game has been used to give a group of production managers a foreknowledge of what it would be like to operate a completely new kind of plant, using a new technology. This not only gave them much help, but meant that they were able to make suggestions for improvements in the plant before it was even built. It has also been used to give managers within a market distribution system prior experience of a new way of calling up consumer goods from the factory to the retail outlets. There are other contexts too. The process is naturally slower by far than full-scale computer simulation, and it would not be used to work out the basic strategies in the first place. But as a means of exploring a new policy once decided, and of training the people who are going to be concerned in the new development project, the tool may be considered invaluable.

The second special use of simulation is this. It is not enough to evolve a policy that looks reliable in the circumstances that one knows about or can predict; that is what we usually do. But one of the things that keeps the manager awake at night is the thought that his policy may be vulnerable to really unexpected circumstances. Suppose that a competitor launches a new product of which today we have no inkling. Suppose that the government, without warning, were to impose a new tax. Or suppose there are variables in the situation to which no sensible value can be ascribed. In these cases simulation is used to discover how vulnerable a policy is to unexpected assault. For the manager wants a policy that is not only profitable, but one that is *robust*. Indeed, it seems realistic to suggest that he does not necessarily want the *most* profitable policy, if this is really rather insecure. He would prefer to trade a little of the profit for a guarantee of stability. All this can be investigated through the simulation by moving certain critical variables around, and especially by moving them *outside* the range of variation that is expected from past performance. Again we see where the system breaks down. This may help the manager to direct research, to plan new developments, to seek new business collaborators, and to form coalitions.

By this point we are beginning to discover the real value of models. Especially note this point. A model is not *just* something that the scientist devises to help him solve a management problem and then throws away, like the sheets of paper on which he has been scribbling mathematics. Insofar as the model has been validated as a representation of some aspect of the firm's activity, it is an asset that the firm has bought. It can be interrogated, really rather quickly, next week—when a new question has arisen. Moreover, if the model is continuously updated by the firm's experience, it is not only an asset, but a growth asset. This can be done by having the model reexamined every six months (say), so that new data may be incorporated in the computer programs. But a better way is to incorporate what can only be called *learning* facilities in the model. This means that what is happening to the firm also happens to the model, which is organized to adapt itself on the strength of its own

Certain management policies—stretching of credit resources, for example —may lead to great progress in good conditions; but, like the Grand Prix car in comparison with the Land Rover, they may not be robust enough to survive when the going gets tough.

experience. This is an especially difficult matter to explain, but it can be done. These are the fruits of cybernetic science again, deriving from studies of how living creatures absorb and use experiential information.

To sum up: The operational research model is a representation of the dynamic system underlying the situation being studied. It is expressed in the rigorous terms of a scientific understanding of some other system to which the situation is being formally analogized. Once the validity of this process has been established (and this can, of course, be done only within certain prescribed limits), then the effort begins to pay off. For all the insights, all the tricks that science has discovered in relation to the type of system being used as a conceptual model, can be imported to the scientific model. It then at once goes to work on the managerial situation.

The importation of all this structure, and in particular the relevant language, is particularly valuable to managers who are willing to learn about it. We really are short of a rich vocabulary of words and ideas when it comes to discussing managerial problems. Most of those we have are taken from economics; and the repeated discussion of management problems in economic terms has led many to imagine that these problems must be in some fundamental sense economic problems. But without minimizing the importance of finance in all human enterprise, it must be true to say that the economic filter on one's spectacles is not the only possible filter. In management science, with its interdisciplinary operational research team, we are thinking essentially in terms of a multi-dimensional model, for the scientific descriptions of natural systems that we borrow *have* to take account of many dimensions at once.

The other general remark about models which should be made is that because they are rigorous and likely to be expressed in mathematical language, they are not therefore necessarily mathematical models. A mathematical model itself is to be found by peering into the box marked T (page 69)—the armory of techniques that the scientists' technical competence has devised for applying the results of scientific modeling to outcomes for the manager. No: The basic nature of a scientific model is *systemic*, rather than mathematical. Plato's *Republic* is what Plato had to say about politics, whether we read it in Greek or in English. We do not make the mistake of saying that the *essence* of this work is to be Greek or English or even to be verbal at all. Equally, the essence of the scientific model is to account for the managerial system, and not to be mathematical.

Here is a final point. We said in the last chapter that the calculus of decision enabled us to compute management strategies *once the manager had stated the level of risk he would accept.* You may well have thought this to be all very well. Suppose that the manager replies: " It is precisely my problem to discover what level of risk I ought to accept." We now have the answer to this difficulty too, because the acceptable level of risk is the most economic level that can be adopted without throwing the rest of the system into uncontrollable oscillation. We can find this out by working on the model of the whole system in terms of its stability.

4 An Alphabet of Models

Nature is an indivisible unit; but man's way of investigating nature is compartmentalized. It is more or less inevitable, then, that the scientific model in an operational research study should be drawn from a particular science. The more one notes this, the more its understanding of system turns out to be indivisible—if one can get over the differences of language and conventions of expression used in the various sciences. The unity of the systemic character of nature is being realized in science today in terms of a body of knowledge called General Systems Theory. Ultimately, perhaps, this new discipline will provide most of the raw material needed by management science for its model-building activity.

In the meantime, operational research has no choice but to use men trained in particular sciences for the work of management science. But since one can never say in advance which science will offer the best (that is to say, most useful, most readily handled) model of a situation, it has remained characteristic of the work that its teams of scientists should be interdisciplinary. You will

A triple modeling process. The dynamics of flow of gas or liquid in various shaped passages can be used to do the computations in a "hydraulic computer," which in turn may be solving a problem in management.

remember the point; it has been made twice before. As a result, an intimate acquaintance with management science reveals a very rich collection of conceptual models. In much operational research reported as such, the conceptual insights provided from other sciences are too often suppressed, and lost in the mathematical apparatus of the rigorous version of the model. Perhaps some work has suffered on this account. At any rate, there are plenty of examples left where the full process described in the last chapter can be examined, and here I shall offer a few of them. These have to be arbitrarily chosen; so just for fun I shall start to construct an ABC of model-building.

A: Acoustics

If, in a well-balanced system that is running satisfactorily, some strange, unpredicted intervention occurs, then it might be described as arriving with a thump. This thump will reverberate around the system. For example, it may be necessary suddenly to introduce an unplanned component of the order book into a smoothly planned production program. Or an unexpected consignment of goods may arrive in a network of warehouses in a distribution system, causing reverberations again. All sorts of sciences, ranging from engineering to psychiatry, can give some account of what happens to a system that is disturbed in this way. But we did say that the disturbance arrived " with a thump." So let us begin the alphabet of models with A for Acoustics.

The problem was this. A complicated arrangement of production processes, all intimately interacting with each other, fed material continuously around the plant. The plant produced a fairly steady, and very low, level of defectives. But every so often, apparently at random, there would be a big surge in the defective rate. The technical people could not trace this to its source. Various possible causes were known, but these were all supposed to be taken care of by elaborate rules for setting the machinery. Now it often happens that an apparently technical problem with no apparent technical solution in a works turns out to be a problem of control.

From time to time in this system, the even flow of production was then interrupted by the need to accommodate material unexpectedly from another plant. This was the thump. The process

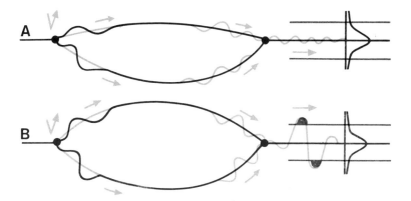

Propagation of a " thump." In the top drawing a disturbance introduced at A travels paths of different length and arrives at point B " out of phase " so that the two parts almost cancel each other. In the bottom drawing the " thump " travels paths of equal length and the two parts arrive at B simultaneously, creating a disturbance of a magnitude beyond that of tolerable limits.

at which this material entered had a good deal of spare capacity, so it had been assumed that the practice was sound. But attention was called to the fact that something atypical occurred at these moments, and the management scientist began to suspect that reverberations from these thumps caused the trouble.

In acoustics, the material surrounding a source of sound will absorb and reflect that sound to a greater or lesser extent. Yes: The analogy works. The processes surrounding this production process absorbed the thump made by the arrival of this extraneous material more or less well, depending on the amount of unutilized production capacity in each place. In acoustics, there is a measurable absorption coefficient for any material; so by analogy we can create a measure to be called an *absorption coefficient* for all the production processes surrounding the one where this intervention takes place. It is the proportion of spare capacity. We also know the speed at which the " sound of the thump " is promulgated. This depends on the rate at which the new material is carried to various processes thereafter. The beginnings of a conceptual model are apparent. In fact, it was possible to make it rigorous.

The behavior of the production system when described in terms of the acoustical model fitted the facts quite well. Now it is well known that the sounds produced in a particular acoustic context will generate " beat " frequencies. The waves of sound reverberate and, as it were, begin to overlap. By investigating the model, such resonances were predicted in the production system, and the job now was to trace them on the shop floor. It sounds extraordinary; and no one had noticed any such subtle phenomena. But now we knew what we were looking for, and we found it. The reverberations of the thump were passing around the system in different directions; so that although on paper there was always spare capacity to accommodate material passed on from another process, overlaps—or beats—were occurring. The effect was that the flow of material " juddered " in a particular process when particular conditions of " resonance " were fulfilled. Thus although this process appeared to be obeying the technical regulations laid down for it, it was not.

Because of the argument about the uniformity of nature and its pervasion systemic laws, it seems entirely likely that some other scientific model would have predicted the same effects. Moreover, they might have been detected by observational studies. The fact is, however, that they were not. It took the use of this model of the control strategy to find the answer. So although this system was not actually an acoustic system, the mapping worked.

B: Biology

Next, consider the famous issue of the optimal size for a firm. Descriptive disciplines, such as economics, have thrown considerable light on the question; especially it is obvious that there is no unique conclusion. Every firm has its own special characteristics, and every environment of a firm has special features too. It is the interaction of the organism and the environment that determines the optimal size for the organism itself. Interruption: Just look at that last sentence again. I am describing this problem as if we had already agreed on a conceptual model of it. The scientist's processes are not so very strange after all; we use analogies all the time as if other people would understand them. They do—because the analogies basically work. There is some sense in which any system can be mapped onto any other.

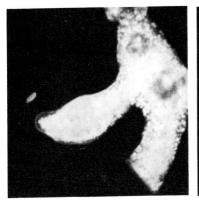
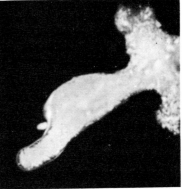
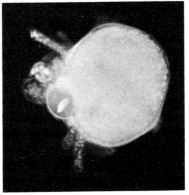

Interaction of a system (an amoeba) with its environment. The amoeba receives a message, presumably chemical in its nature, telling it that a food particle is present. The amoeba reacts by engulfing the particle.

It seems we have arrived in the alphabet of models at B for Biology. And why should we not talk about the firm as a viable organism? If it is, then the first thing biology has to say is that there must be a very rich interaction between a living cell and the stuff outside it. Even at the conceptual level of modeling, this is quite a thought. We tend to think of a firm as having rather tenuous connections with the outside world. There is a thin stream of orders reaching it from its market, and a thin stream of goods flowing outward. There is information going out with the goods—instructions, publicity, and so forth. There is information coming back—in the form of reorders (satisfied customers), complaints, and so on. But this stylized account of the interaction is completely inadequate. Every employee of the firm represents his firm in some milieu or another. There are a whole lot of social interactions going on that we normally ignore. And there are more complicated interactions between the firm and its customers in their use of the product than might at first be suspected.

How important is all this? The answer is: very important. There is a mechanism called *osmosis* that connects the interior to the exterior of the living cell. Information, in chemically coded form, passes back and forth through the cell's walls on a very big scale. There are feedback arrangements implicit in this chemistry of osmotic flow that cause the cell to grow to its optimal size and not to exceed it. In the rigorous model, we shall want to import from biology the diffusion equations that describe all this. When this has been done, it will be possible to identify in industrial terms the structural components of the comparable feedback that supplies the size determinants of the firm.

Think for a moment of the relevance of this model to problems of national productive capacities and *their* size. How big should productive capacity be in a primary industry such as steel, for example? We already try to measure this through (an unrecognized) model of osmosis. For steel in many shapes and forms works out through the " cell walls " of the industry into many markets and uses, carrying information about the industry with it. This information is about quality, price, and so forth; it is also about the length of delivery promises, and the industry's capacity to meet them. The information fed back by the hierarchy of markets is difficult indeed to interpret. The secondary industries, which reroll and forge and draw steel, want supplies—and they will not be carrying very much stock. *Their* customers may carry more stock, and so on down the chain. By the time we get to finished products made of anything but steel, but incorporating steel components, no one can say what the effect of the diffused information has become, nor how to interpret the information diffusing back. The whole picture is complicated by the stockists and merchants who will try to exploit any shortages that may appear.

The result is this. The fedback information from the industry's environment consists, first and foremost, of a forward order load. Much of this " demand for steel " will be bogus. Because everyone

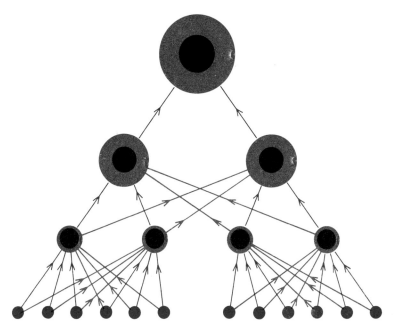

Multiplication of spurious demand. Each of the twelve customers (bottom row), fearing a shortage, places his order with two different suppliers. The suppliers in turn place their orders in duplicate with two different manufacturers. The resulting apparent demand (red plus black) is four times the actual demand (black).

in the chain of supply is seeking to protect himself, he places long-term orders with more than one supplier—many of which he will subsequently cancel. The industry adds up the total of all its orders, and finds it has inadequate capacity. So it embarks on new capital investment; and it meanwhile rations steel. This causes, through the lagged feedback system, further alarm in the markets, which may soon order still more unwanted material. In Britain this collapse of the biochemical-type control of the organism's size has caused a lot of difficulty. It makes the economic assessment of the nation's need impossible. Above all, to take the argument further, if an expansion in a *user* industry is required for the national good (in machine tools, for instance) it becomes totally impossible to work out—backward through the system of biochemical feed-back—what changes in primary steelmaking capacity are required. Merely economic models are (and have been demonstrated in practice to be) no good. The biological model, with its potentiality to account for the complicated informational circuits involved, is required.

C: Cybernetics

But enough of the letter B. The alphabet goes on. C is for Cybernetics, the science of control, which supplies a steady stream of models for the management scientist. The more we learn about control systems in nature, and especially in conscious animals, and above all in their brains, the more we begin to understand how the organism learns from its own experience, seeks and finds a goal, settles down again after being disturbed, adapts to different stimuli, and evolves to meet changing circumstances. In a word, we begin to understand what the mechanism of survival is. All this information is valuable to the firm, which has to meet all these problems too—and especially the last.

For example, the brain is able to give coherent decisions despite the inherent unreliability of its components—which is high. Indeed, not only are brain cells unreliable, not only are they unreliably connected, they even pack up altogether at an alarming rate. It is estimated that we lose 100,000 brain cells a day throughout our lives—and this is rather a lot, even though there are ten thousand million such cells in our heads. We have only (say) 70 per cent of them left by the time we are seventy. But the neuro-physiologist knows how the brain does the trick of getting reliable decisions out of such a rickety organization. It is basically by using many different channels and many different cells to do the same thing, and cross-feeding the answers. The cybernetician has borrowed a neurophysiological model to evolve a rigorous theory about the reliability and optimal structure of decision-taking systems. No wonder, then, that the management scientist uses a cybernetic model to discuss company organizations. It is very rewarding.

Notice how much more realistic is this model than the one management usually uses: the organizational chart modeled on the family tree. That model is all right as a way of defining rank and

A single neuron (nerve cell) showing the termination of numerous dendrites from other cells upon its surface.

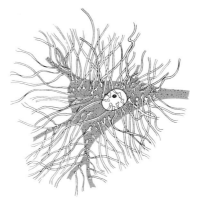

fundamental chains of command. But it really tells us nothing we may want to know about the way the system works, or ought to work; nor does it convey any hints about the reliability of the system and of its workings. Yet, after all, the manager too is a fallible creature. He may even pack up like a defunct brain cell. So, as illustrated, we use cybernetic models to investigate the structure of management itself.

In this much over-simplified case, we see a single brain cell, which has (let us say) a probability of going wrong of 1-in-200. So it is 0·995 reliable. It is fed with information from two sources (the simplest case), each of which is wrong for 30 per cent of the time. These inputs, then, are each reliable with a probability of 0·7. Suppose that the cell has to decide to act, represented by firing its axon, when both inputs simultaneously say that it should. Before going on, let us note how this situation models a manager trying to reach a decision. He has two assistants (Parkinson's Law), each giving him 70 per cent good information—not a bad rate. He himself makes a mistake once in two hundred times. Well, he is only human. The model holds.

We now ask what is the probability of getting the *wrong* answer in these very particular circumstances. All three parts of the system must operate correctly, and at once, if the answer is going to be correct. This is a multiplicative probability: $0·7 \times 0·7 \times 0·995$. If we subtract the answer to that from unity, we have the chance of going wrong. The probability of being wrong, then, is 0·51245—51 per cent, or more than an even chance. But here is a point. How can one be systematically—on the average—*wrong* in these circumstances? If we invite this manager to consider his input information with great care, and to use all his knowledge and experience to evaluate it, he will be wrong more than half the time. So the best advice for him is to take his decision with every care—and then reverse it. He will thus be *right* for most of the time. This mechanism would make a mockery of management, and a mockery of our own brains as well. And yet the basic figures look reasonable both to the neurophysiologist and to the management observer. The answer is that the brain uses a redundant organizational structure, such as that shown. Here there are three brain cells (all still making mistakes); each cell has two inputs, as before, but now each input has five separate channels, all equally unreliable. It would appear that the answers would be even more unreliable than before, but this is not so. An organization of this kind has the following probability of going wrong:

$$P = \left[1 - (1 - 0 \cdot 3^5)\,(0 \cdot 995)\right]^4 = 3 \cdot 03 \times 10^{-9}$$

Now we have a risk of error in the region of one in a hundred million. This is a considerable improvement on our earlier result. We have actually managed to amplify the reliability of decision enormously.

I have tried to make this example lighthearted, but the principles are perfectly correct. The cybernetic model shows management organizers the *quantified* way to discuss structure. It seems to me that every competent manager knows in general that this is how organizations really work. Decisions are taken in consultation, not alone. Information is sought, perhaps unofficially, from many sources—not only from one's own official subordinates. Yet the official texts on the theory of management try to describe organizations in terms of a family tree, and real-life managers hang these inadequate models on their walls. The new cybernetic model is a neurophysiological mapping of the way things really are. It gives a logic and a decision calculus for working out good management structures, too. This is of real use.

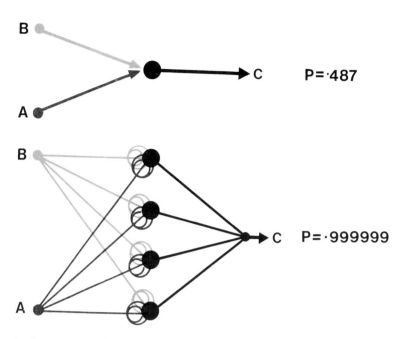

C   P=·487

C   P=·999999

In these systems there should be an output pulse at C when pulses arrive at the processing center (black circle) from both A and B. As explained in the text, the redundant system, (lower part of the diagram) is almost certain to function correctly, because all the signal paths are duplicated several times.

D: Demography

D is for Demography, the science that deals with birth and death processes in a population. Just contemplate for a moment the comparison between a population of people and a population of machines that go to make up a plant. Both are born, and both grow to maturity. (Do we not even say that a new machine has " teething troubles?") Both men and machines have a useful working life, and then begin increasingly to fail, increasingly to need more maintenance. In the end both suffer from obsolescence—and ultimately die. Somewhere in this process both need to have components replaced, and both may require fundamental

The steam railway engine being scrapped in the photograph above is not defective or worn out; it is simply unprofitable to operate any longer, because of the amount and type of maintenance required. The modern diesel-electric engine operates with a smaller crew and less maintenance.

surgery. At another point in the process both spawn. The man begets progeny that mature in time for him to sink into a decline. The machine also (through research and development) embarks on a second generation while still in the prime of life. This conceptual model has been made rigorous too. For there is a whole mathematical theory to deal with these demographic phenomena, and this has been transported into the industrial situation as well. Here again, then, is a valuable model. It has relevance to maintenance policies, and particularly to preventive maintenance; to research and development; to investment policy; and it even extends, through these things, to product policy as well.

We have spoken, in A to D above, of production processes, of the size of firms and industrial capacities, of management structure, and of the plant itself. It is time to mention marketing. We know that markets buy the things that factories make, and that factories make the things that markets buy. There is a loop here; it is closed. This is the language of servomechanics, a branch of E for Engineering.

E: Engineering

Now the important thing about the two-way interaction between supply and demand is its dynamics. That is to say, this is not a static relationship; the loop goes around and around as time unfolds. What matters most to the company is that it should not have to find a completely new customer to stand for the market on each circuit. It wants a loyal customer, one who buys again. In the language of engineering, then, there is a feedback here, and that is what provides the closed loop. When feedbacks do not operate as they should, which happens because the control engineering has not been properly done, the whole system goes into oscillation. We discussed this pervasive feedback mechanism in the biological example. Now it arises in its own engineering terms.

Has proper control engineering been done on the purchase-repurchase feedback loop of the company's marketing situation? This becomes the question. It can be done, of course; because this conceptual model can be translated into a scientific model, and really sensitive controls can be installed. But in the customary absence of this work of management science, the mechanism operates because the company has acquired skill over the years in making it work. But despite this, the absence of good control theory is likely to mean that even an experienced management will be unable to stop the system from oscillating from time to time. That is a prediction from the model; and we ought to ask whether the prediction is borne out or falsified in practice.

The situation is familiar enough. There is a run on stocks of a certain commodity. Rapid alterations are made in the production plan to reinforce them. The demand curve is rising, and the sales department extrapolates it into the future. The stocks surge up. Then, unaccountably, there is a sudden cessation in demand. The rate of increase in the size of stock increases. Somebody cries: " Stop production." There is a pause while the stocks are consumed; and no one will stick his neck out by building them up again too soon after the last scare. When the next surge in demand occurs, the panic starts again. In engineering terms, the system is *hunting*.

With the control theory model from servomechanics, a

Uncontrolled marketing feedback (in France in 1962) resulted in the supply of artichokes quite literally " flooding the market "—as shown in the photo.

managerial filter is placed between the feedback circuit from the sales end (where supply and demand are actually compared) and the production end (where the rate of input has to be decided). According to the basic mathematics of servo theory, the incorporation of such a filter makes the control of production flow virtually independent of arbitrary movements in demand. Moreover, the model can prescribe the characteristics that the filter should have.

Having got this far, the management scientist is left with the problem of designing the filter in management terms. There are various ways of doing this, and the best known of them has been elevated to the status of a special operational research technique. It is called *exponential smoothing*. All this means is that the production flow is adjusted not from moment to moment by every variation in the market, but by a rather complicated amalgam of recent experience. The effect of this is to attach quite a lot of weight to what the market is now doing, but not much less to what it was doing in the previous epoch; and a little less than that weight is

If weekly sales reports are fed back directly to the production manager, output is likely to fluctuate wildly as the factory tries to follow random fluctuations in demand. Inserting a management filter in the feedback loop, to interpret the market reports, results in a more smoothly operating system.

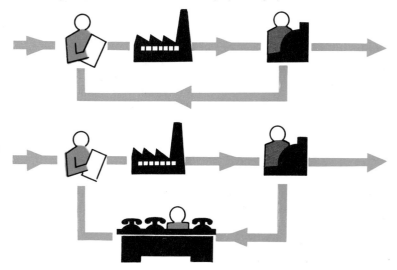

attached to the market's behavior in the epoch before that; and so on. Thus the further back in time one goes, the less effect does the market's behavior then have on one's present actions. Or, to put it the other way round, the market's present behavior will have a decaying effect on production policy for a long time to come.

You see why the operation of this filter is called a " smoothing " operation. The reason why it is called " exponential " is that this is the name of the mathematical curve that decaying processes normally follow in nature. The charge on a condenser decays like this (P for Physics, perhaps). The number of people off work sick at the peak of an epidemic also decays like this as they gradually return to work (E for Epidemiology). This model of a process that decays can be taken from almost any science: We again face a natural law of system. In this case, it fits into a model from engineering.

Please note in passing that we have once again stumbled on a technique of operational research that has often been lifted out of its proper context, which is the servomechanistic model. The technique of exponential smoothing has been packaged, and sold as a job lot. The trouble is, as usual, that although the idea of using the technique in such circumstances as those described is quite generally sound, there is no means of knowing what the weights ought to be unless the characteristics of the filter in the servo-system have first been understood. This means deploying the whole model and the whole system—not just playing about with it.

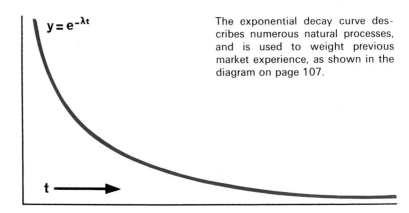

$$y = e^{-\lambda t}$$

The exponential decay curve describes numerous natural processes, and is used to weight previous market experience, as shown in the diagram on page 107.

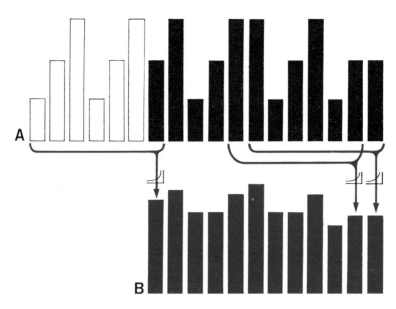

A smoothed demand curve. The raw sales reports for 17 months are shown at the top. The smoothed curve representing production orders for the past 12 months is below. It is derived from the sales report by assigning the current sales report a weight of one, last month's report a weight of ·83, and so on until the report of six months ago has a prediction of ·05.

F: Fluid Dynamics

But all this industrial talk becomes boring; let us turn briefly to another sort of management, for a break. Problems of traffic are becoming so severe in many countries that whole transportation systems threaten to seize up. Now traffic on the roads constitutes a flow. The flow is made up of individual vehicles, it is true. But it is a common trick in science to treat something made up of many or few individual things as if it were a more or less dense continuous substance. C for Cosmology does this when it discusses the distribution of matter in distant space. The point may be slightly baffling, but it is really just a question of what sort of mathematical description is most readily used.

So a " stream " of traffic down a road (again the conceptual model is second nature) may be analogized to a liquid. This liquid moves at a rate; it is more or less viscose. All the right scientific terms apply in a very obvious way, and we have the classic model (developed by Professor Lighthill) from F for Fluid Dynamics. A lot of information was gleaned about the effects of narrowing and widening roads, and of instituting traffic lights.

It was found that both these forms of affecting flow caused shock waves to pass backward through the traffic, just as they would through liquid—although traffic engineers knew this already. What the model predicted that was novel, however, was the propagation of secondary shock waves, the existence of which had not been suspected. But they were found all right, afterward. This work has been used to help make decisions about networks of roads and their control. But as anyone can see, all the more highly industrialized nations of the world have a lot more use to make of management science than this when it comes to transportation policies.

G: Genetics

We may now turn back, refreshed, to the problems of the firm. How many salesmen does a firm need? This depends on their efficiency, on their taking the most productive route around their territory, and on the excellence of the psychology underlying their briefing for the approach to the market. All three of these things

A slowly moving queue does not move uniformly. Rather, waves of motion pass down the queue. The frequency and amplitude of these waves is inversely related to the speed at which the queue is served.

have been studied by management science. But assuming such matters to be held constant, there is another interesting factor to consider. The salesman does not make an impact that stops dead; his customer speaks to another. He makes a thump that reverberates, if you like. Or to use another analogy, and to invoke another conceptual model, the salesman initiates a breeding process. We cannot now go back through the alphabet to A for Acoustics. We have reached G—G for Genetics.

The strides made by the science of genetics in recent years have been enormous. A great new understanding has developed of the processes involved, and with it have come the usual rigorous descriptions that the management scientist can borrow. So the salesmen are seen as initiating a process of reproduction, and the way the territory is covered can be analyzed in genetic terms. There comes a point when it does not pay to have any more salesmen, whatever one might think from a raw comparison of their number with the target population of potential customers. But perhaps the point about models has been taken, without our going into more detail in this particular case.

We have had seven examples of scientific models, after all, and a number of sidelights as well. Acoustics, Biology, Cybernetics, Demography, Engineering, Fluid Dynamics, and Genetics make quite a list of creditor sciences as it stands. Perhaps we should try to take the alphabet on to Hydraulics and Immunology, but although I could deal with the first of these factually, I should have to make

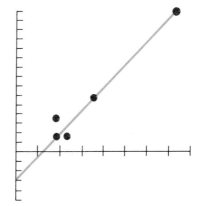

The growth of a company predicted from the ratio of number of salesmen to present share of the market. The solid line represents the prediction, from a model derived from genetics; dots represent the actual experience.

the second example up. *So far I have given only such illustrations as are within my own experience of actual cases.* Sometimes, you will note, the studies involved are of a kind that leads to savings—and savings have been made. Sometimes they lead only to the advice that yields a less risky decision, a better policy, or a much more potent control. I say " only." For it is gratifying, and tidy, and moreover convincing, to quote actual savings. But the other things are doubly important. Perhaps one day the accountant will arise capable of calculating the benefits of such successes of management science as these. In the meantime, it does not really need much imagination to see how we may get a grasp of the underlying system that generates profit, and make it work.

Models and Mapping

So this alphabet gives out, far short of Z for Zoology; but the joke wearies and the space runs out. I hope the point is made, however, because it would be useful now to consider a little more carefully the question of how a model is to be mapped. We need rather more understanding of this as a practical method than has so far been provided. The point involved is this. Some way back we grappled with those two ugly words *isomorphism* and *homomorphism*. We then understood, but may since have forgotten, that the models under discussion are essentially homomorphic. In mapping themselves onto reality, that is, they preserve those structural facts that are important to the problem, but they make life easier by transforming the elements of the real-life system onto a many-to-one basis. The point I want to discuss can be summed up by asking: *how* many to one?

It is evident that if one stands a long way from something that is going on, one loses a lot of the finer detail. But it may be possible to detect gross changes nonetheless. We can say, if we like, that last year's expenses were so many million dollars and last year's income was so many million (we hope this figure is larger), whereas this year the two figures are somewhat different. This enables us to calculate the profit in both years, and to declare that the company is improving or declining in profitability. There is not much perception of detail in this, but the conclusions are important. If we want to know *why* the changes are as they are, we shall have to go a

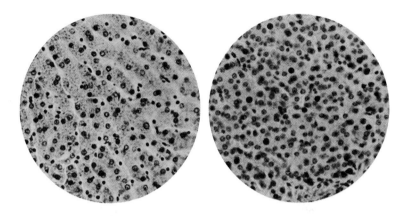

The photo (left) is liver tissue from a pig; that on the right liver tissue from a man; both × 32. This scale of resolution is excellent for studying " liver," but quite inappropriate to studying essential differences between man and pig.

bit closer. We may bring the market into focus, so that different geographical areas or different sets of products are detected, and more judgments can be made. So the resolution of the situation can go on. We adjust the lens in order to see more or less detail as required. This suggests that the many-to-oneness of a model is an arbitrary matter, calling upon the management scientist to reach his decision on the strength of what he is trying to find out.

The Cones of Resolution

Here we have yet another model—this time of an aspect of the management science methodology itself. Yet again we see that we are turning naturally to a particular science—for a conceptual model of the modeling process itself. O is for Optics, and words such as focus and resolution have already become useful. In the diagram we see the old picture of the company interacting with its market, and *every* degree of coarseness and fineness in the modeling possibilities is in principle shown. This claim can be made because we start with a pinpoint model at the top, having no resolution, and end with the fully resolved complexity of real life at

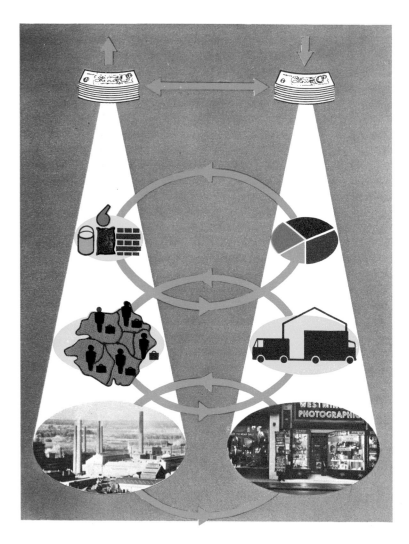

For some purposes comparison of cash income with expense (top level) adequately describes the interaction of a company with its market. For other purposes the proportion of income derived from each product is relevant, for others the number of trade representatives, etc., is required, and so on down the cone of resolution until we come to the actual company and market.

the bottom. Every level of resolution must be passed on the way down. I call this picture the *cones of resolution.*

If we sit at the apex of either of the two cones, our model is very-very-many-to-one, for we are left with two points, each of which is said to be interacting with the other. This is not much use, unless the value attached to each point is known. As mentioned just now, there is an example of this: the profit and loss account. The single point representing the market has a measure attached to it: turnover. So this ultimately simple model is the one that tells us the profit. As we work down through the two cones of resolution, we get more and more understanding of what is really happening. If we hit the ground, we encounter the uniquely isomorphic model: the company itself interacting with the market itself. This is not much use to us either, because the only way to play the game at this ultimate level of modeling is to continue managing the situation as it is.

Clearly, the most economic way to do management science is to stay as high up in the cone of resolution as one can. The pinpoint model at the top of the cones of resolution can be created for a given company at lunch, on the back of an envelope, by asking the financial director what the figures are. As the scientist descends the cone in his search for understanding of the total system, his task gets bigger and bigger. Now there is a special trick about handling this expanding task. The thing to do is to start with a modestly sized model of low resolution that can be constructed in a week or so. By working with this model (perhaps by analysis, perhaps by simulation) one begins to learn, even at this coarse level, what areas or subsystems of the activities under study are relatively unimportant. This is discoverable by varying the values of their key variables, and seeing whether the variation has much effect on the total outcome.

Some boxes representing subsystems in the model will, on the contrary, have an enormous effect on the outcome. These are the ones it is vital to know more about. Therefore the scientist descends the cone of resolution a little further, but only in those boxes that are important. This means to say that when he comes to build a more elaborate model lower down the cone, he no longer has the entire field of operations to consider. He has left the uninteresting

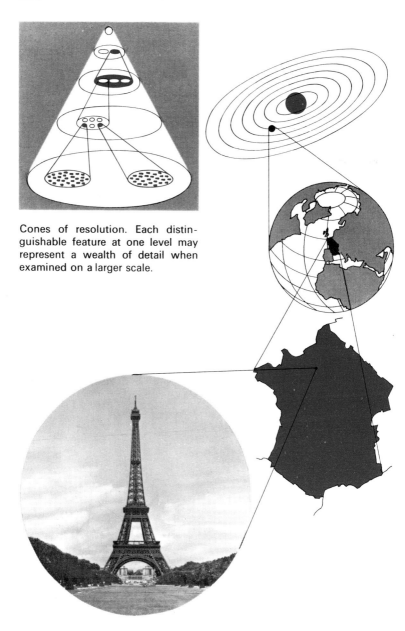

Cones of resolution. Each distinguishable feature at one level may represent a wealth of detail when examined on a larger scale.

one behind. The same thing happens once more. Given more resolution still, he gets more detail still, and again he may discover that parts of the subsystem he has uncovered are relatively unimportant, while other parts remain important and obscure. And so on, right down the cone.

It is terribly important to appreciate that some things remain obscure to the bitter end. In these cases the scientist actually hits the ground. And this is where the old-fashioned empirical research really begins, because he is now operating on the isomorphic model of reality—reality itself. The scientist will have to get out and discover what is happening. He will probably get very dirty. But the task is worthwhile, and it is economic to his employers. For he will not be embarking on the hopeless task of making a complete analysis of the whole isomorphic model at ground level. He will be studying only those bits of it that are critical to the homomorphic models higher up. Thus he may want to undertake market research in certain specialized areas for certain specialized products, and even to undertake depth psychology on particular transactions. He could not do this for the entire range of products in the entire markets of the company: It would be ruinously expensive. Again he may call for detailed work studies of *particular* operations in the factory. And so on.

All this means that the management scientist is likely to end up with a hierarchy of models rather than one model. His first model is coarse, his second finer, and so on down. The finer models deal with parts of systems, and lock into coarser and more complete models higher up the cone. In the next chapter, we shall proceed to look at just two very important problems of management. These will be illustrated (as usual) by actual examples—names being omitted or changed. But this time it will not be a question of showing how models operate alone; we shall see how problems arise and are solved. We shall also see how the whole methodology, which has now been explained, actually works.

You may be taking (and deserve) a rest before embarking on the new chapter. If so, remember that I owe you an illustration of these last arguments. Please do not forget about the cones of resolution.

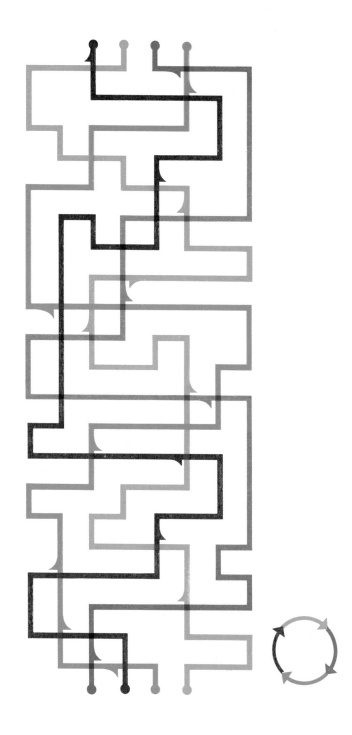

5 It Works

Management problems are not respecters of the company organization, nor of the talents of the people appointed to solve them. What at first appears to be a stockbroking problem rooted in the works may hinge on demand forecasting out in the market. Equally, what seems to be a marketing question, such as the number of lines of a product that ought to be sold, may have more to do with production than the sales director thinks. For the marketing policy about the number of lines is worked out in terms of the cost at which the goods can be made available from the factory. This presupposes that the factory's costs are independent of the product mix; but they are not.

Try to visualize the following exercise. We pretend that the market will buy whatever we make. And what shall we make? We want to find the best possible use for our assets of plant and machinery: We want a product mix that will keep all the machinery utilized all the time. This also enables us to make the very best use of the labor force, which can be tailored to suit this optimal plan.

A typical minimization problem is to find the shortest path from top to bottom. Transferring at intersections is allowed only as indicated by the circle (bottom right). The problem, though trivial, is of a type best handled by a computer.

The remaining major component of cost is raw material, so let us minimize the expense in this as well. What is happening here is that all the resources at the management's command are being permuted. The object is to settle on the least costly production program that will manufacture any output that keeps all the resources going without waste.

The job is not as easy to do as it sounds, because of the huge variety of possible programs and process routes that could be used. Everything has to be right at once, and the permutations seem endless. But if we are clever with the mathematics of the situation it can be done. It is clear, for instance, that many of the possible programs we suggest can be eliminated forthwith, because they would be more expensive than some other program we have already listed. Eventually we can spot the winning arrangement, simply because the sole rule of the game is that minimum cost wins.

Let us take our results to the sales director. He is going to get quite a shock when he sees what a strange collection of products, and in what disbalanced quantities, we should like him to sell. But he will get another, and much more pleasant, shock when he finds out what the costs of these things are. It must be nearly fifteen years since I first did this particular trick, in a light-engineering works, but I remember as if it were yesterday the consternation. This was already an extremely profitable place; yet the result of the exercise showed a possible increase in profit of more than 500 per cent.

What should the management do now? Insist that the sales side sells this particular mixture of products and no other? But this is impracticable. In the first place, agreements may have been made to supply more of one product than the optimal program allows to be made. Or perhaps we need to make and sell a loss-bearing line in order to achieve other orders that are highly profitable. Well, we can do the whole exercise again, putting in these practical marketing constraints. This means expressing the mathematics in such a way that we find the best production arrangement *subject to* fulfilling agreements, making a reasonable range available, and so forth. Even this is likely to result in a much enhanced profit over the one we started with. But the real benefit of all this work is to explore what the situation is like. There are at least three very important and sensible things that management can do, even if it

Part of a more practical minimization problem. The diagram shows the flow of iron ore (sea-borne only) in the Atlantic area. The problem, of course, is to produce the right amount of iron at each processing plant with minimum cost. This problem is complicated by the fact that the ore-carriers require a cargo in the opposite direction to operate most profitably, by the fact that the finished product (pig-iron) can be carried more economically than raw ore, and by currency restrictions, customs, conventional markets, etc.

assumes that no radical change is possible in normal business activity, by changing its own policy. The first is to pursue nearly optimal programs of production, manufacturing for stock. The impact of fluctuating demands can then to some extent be absorbed—and of course in a predictable way, thanks to the statistical treatment of this problem as a stochastic process. The stock needed costs money; but that can be evaluated too, and examined in relation to the potential profits of the scheme. The second strategy augments the first. Because we intend to manufacture nearly optimal programs, we expect to make a much higher profit. Some of this return can be used to reduce selling prices differentially. This will have the effect of conditioning the market to buy what it most pays to sell. The third strategy that a management can adopt is not often contemplated, because of the gulf that customarily separates production and sales management. It is this. We can change our investment in the plant itself, altering the balance of machinery until the optimal arrangement is roughly equivalent to the demand forecast from the market. Then we shall have the best of both worlds.

The mathematical technique that backs up this work is called linear programming. We can regard each possible program as a line; every line is in reality a linear equation, because it proposes a particular mixture of resources that adds up to the total resources available. Equally, every line yields a selection of possible outputs. Every equation in the system has to be written to take account of the agreed restraints. After this, the task is very like solving all these equations simultaneously. You will not have forgotten, from school algebra, that to solve a simultaneous equation means having as many equations as there are unknowns. In linear programming this condition is probably not fulfilled : Therefore there are a whole lot of possible answers that would work. These are called the *feasible solutions* to the program. But, as we said before, we do also have the criterion by which to select just one of these : We want to minimize cost. The final and overriding equation that expresses this desire is called the " optimizing functional." It means that the whole set of simultaneous equations has to be resolved under this very special constraint: " that there is no cheaper answer."

The Limitations of Techniques As Such

Now this very powerful operational research technique is based on a mathematical model. This discusses the way that abstract variables, such as costs, move in relation to each other within a weird kind of abstract space. It is best to distinguish this from the kind of model previously discussed, which is an attempt to map a real-life system onto a scientific analogy of what is actually going

In the highly interrelated biological complex shown below, it is only our particular interest that determines what part we call the " system " and what part we call the environment.

on. Mathematical programming (the equations do not have to be linear), like the technique derived from stochastic processes, is best thought of as one of the techniques by which systemic models may be quantified. Many people have tried to use the mathematical model on its own. To do this, they have to think out how all the variables in the real-life situation are related to each other, and thereby *invent* the substance of the system. This is why many people have had unfortunate experiences with linear programming. The mathematics may be very clever, the variables may be properly listed, and the major constraints may be discovered and applied. But if we consider the mathematics as a model of a real-life situation, we may find that the mapping is not very penetrating into all those complicated interactions that are the elements of what really goes on.

One of the reasons for this is that mathematical programming studies may well be commissioned by one branch of a management, such as production or sales, which will feed the applied mathematician with data that fairly well account for its own activity, but inadequately represent the activities of other branches. Now a management scientist ought not to be taking account of these conventional divisions. Most of the usefulness of an operational research team lies in its ability to make a model of the *whole* (relevant) enterprise. As was seen in the illustration, programming in aid of production may present sales with a nonsense; equivalently, an optimal mix determined in terms of prices and profits under marketing constraints may present production with fantastic costs. Even when the programming is done to balance both sides, it is silly to accept the situation as it is. For the management is there to alter that situation, provided the changes proposed are sensible ones. Thus the scientific modeling process so far discussed in this book, whereby a scientist can search for new and better management strategies, is to be quantified by techniques that, taken alone, are blinkered.

Putting the whole argument together, we see a very exciting prospect ahead. Losses in productivity and unnecessarily high costs, inadequate exploitation of the market and unnecessarily low profits, may be due to quite small gaps in productive and marketing facilities. Because of the way everything is interacting together, these small deficiencies are costing us dear. If they can be remedied, perhaps quite cheaply, we are using investment as a golden key to unlock the entire system. To do so, we must stop thinking of investment simply as a process of increasing or modernizing capacity with the sole aim of " adopting the most modern practice." The first way of looking at investment is as the missing piece in a jigsaw puzzle that suddenly makes sense of the whole thing.

Modeling the Real-life Situation

The account that now follows of all this working in an actual job begins by saying that the original commission was to look at production itself; it was certainly not conceived as an investment study. The operational research team did not know what would come of it either. But here was an enlightened management which knew that there was a problem, and agreed that the use of management science must imply freedom of investigation, and permission to reconsider any of the company's policies. We knew that we were considering an enterprise interacting with various entities outside itself. So the first conceptual model was drawn from ecology, because this is the science that considers an organism interacting with its environment.

When we drew a picture of this situation in the last chapter, we very naturally showed the environment as surrounding the organism. But now the picture separates these two. This is just for future convenience. Certainly, the diagram contains little enough information. It depicts a pinpoint model alone. Some pages have passed since I made my plea to remember the theory of cones of resolution. Now we need this model of how to model. For the degree of resolution so far obtained is virtually nil, and we shall have to find out how to come down the cone of resolution using a *hierarchy* of scientific models.

The satisfactory point about the model so far is that it incorporates a closed loop. Although nothing is ever really isolated from everything else, the model indicates in one fell swoop everything that perceptibly affects the day-to-day operation of the system. All this is asserted to be in one or other of the boxes. So although it is tempting to say that this unresolved picture oversimplifies what is happening, this is not quite right. Simplification often entails

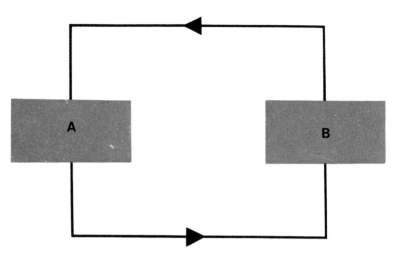

The division of the complex activity into the company (A) and its environment (B) is somewhat arbitrary, but serves as a starting point for the modeling process.

exclusion of things that are relevant, and this can be dangerous. This model is *all*-inclusive, but not elaborated. The boxes are blank; anything may be going on inside them. Once we try to explain the detail inside the box, we shall indeed have to simplify the relationships that arise. But if the resolution of detail is restricted to identification of sub-boxes that are in turn left blank, we shall be able to keep in mind the limited state of our enlarging knowledge, and not jump to conclusions.

The conceptual model from ecology gives us the clue that there are various dimensions of environmental interaction. In a living organism, one can discuss the in-and-out cycle of oxygen, for example, or the ingestion-digestion-excretion cycle of food, or cycles having to do with responses to danger through the endocrine system. Similarly, the business environment may be resolved into a number of dimensions. The *market* for goods is obviously such a dimension; we have talked before about the demand environment, and its purchase-repurchase feedback loop. In the case under consideration, the *supply* environment was also vital, because the raw materials were not things one simply ordered from a

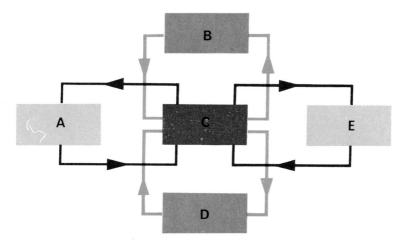

The diagram above, showing the interaction of the company (C) with its supply environment (A), working environment (B), financial environment (D), and demand environment (E) is a further step in the modeling process. It is still significantly oversimplified.

merchant: They had to be especially imported from abroad. So a purchase-use-repurchase feedback cycle became important there. As often happens, the *labor* force offered a number of management problems, and its cycle of interactions with the company constituted another environmental dimension. Finally, various *flows of money* turned out to have an important bearing. Cash flow is always important, because it is a condition of the company's existence that it can convert goods to cash and cash to goods, and that there is an adequate supply of cash. This is very like the oxygen interchange. But in this case there were other financial aspects, including questions about the availability of capital.

So now we have a diagram to show rather more resolution of the environment, and we have begun that empirical investigation into the actual facts without which science is mere daydreaming. The team began also to investigate the internal activity of the company, very largely in terms of the impact of the various dimensions of environment upon it. What came out of the study at this stage was that the financial environment, although terribly important, could be expressed as an integral part of the company's internal activity.

Cash flows themselves are floated on the supply and demand environments; financial operations involving capital will have to be paid for in a very short run out of the revenue accruing over that period. Secondly, the working environment could be similarly treated; factors affecting labor were almost entirely accounted for within the firm itself. (This is not always so. In the case of a dockyard, or any other concern where there is a highly mobile in-and-out flow of seasonal labor, this environmental dimension would certainly have to be modeled on its own.)

In this way the second hierarchical level in the cone of resolution was reached. The supply and demand environments had been examined, and themselves resolved into further boxes. The financial and working environments had been suppressed by incorporating what was relevant about them into the resolved account of the company's internal activity. And now some new model was needed to express all this. The science chosen to depict the interacting system at this level was general systems theory. A diagram showing the relationship implicit in that model may now be studied. Here, the supply environment in the smaller horseshoe is illustrated, together with its three main material sources and their alternatives illustrated. The demand environment, the larger horseshoe, is made up of ten separate markets. It will be noted that these markets allow for the possibility of mixing the firm's products in terms of semi-finished goods as well as total manufactures. We have still attempted no resolution of the boxes, which are blank. But we have gone a long way toward describing the interactions of the system. These could all be statistically quantified in terms of magnitudes, probabilities, and time cycles: stochastic processes are in being.

This means in turn that quite a lot could already be said about the stability of the system, and about the vulnerability of the organism to environmental changes. These conclusions are inferred from the ecological relationships, and not from information about the contents of all the little boxes, which are still unresolved. This is an interesting demonstration of the systematic quality of a system: Its general behavior is determined more by interactions than by the things that interact.

At this degree of resolution, it would be possible to simulate the operation of the system. But, as a matter of fact, the system was

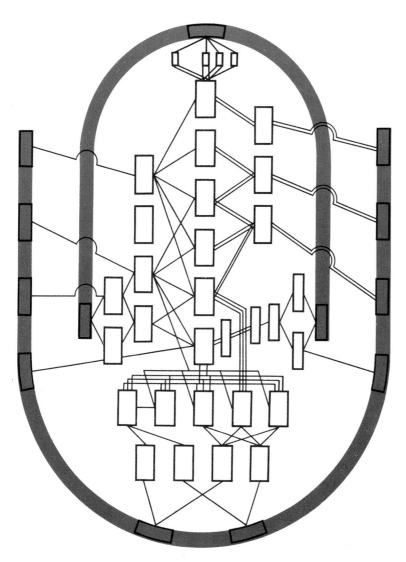

The company-environment interaction further modeled. The two outer segments (brown) represent the demand and the supply environments respectively. The complexity of the situation is becoming more evident in this diagram.

simulating itself rather well, at the isomorphic level. That is to say, the general dynamics of the whole business seemed very well understood. What we wanted to get at were the *decision* elements of the system. Now here we run into difficulties with words if we are not careful. If more than one course of action is open at any given point in the system at any given time, then a decision is required to resolve the alternatives. Sometimes this means that a man must make a choice, which is the ordinary meaning of " taking a decision." But sometimes the system itself effectively makes the choice, because its global state is such that the required decision follows inexorably from the state of affairs that exists elsewhere. We are back with arguments about reverberations and interactions; in a word, we are talking about the *self-organizing* properties of systems.

If you think about it, these properties are the most important decision elements in an enterprise. No manager has time to make conscious, deliberated choices whenever an alternative exists. Management relies more heavily than it often realizes on the system's intrinsic ability to do the right thing—and this includes sensible behavior on the part of workers who know nothing of the company's policies as such. So moving down the cone of resolution, we wanted to resolve the general systems model into another model that would specify the decision properties of the system, and distinguish between the self-organizing ones and those that required managerial intervention. The answers would be required, of course, in quantified form.

So the next model in the hierarchy of models was chosen from electrical engineering. The design of a system in electrical terms guarantees that its decision points are known, and that the information required to run the system is fully specified. To be precise, the model (which is reproduced here) is a servo-mechanism that offers an isomorphic mapping of the earlier model from general systems theory. It is less resolved in terms of its stochastic components, but more resolved in terms of its information flow. Moreover, it is a completely rigorous account of the situation. What we really have at this point is an electrical analogue that would behave exactly like the organic system under study. It could indeed have been constructed in hardware as an analogue

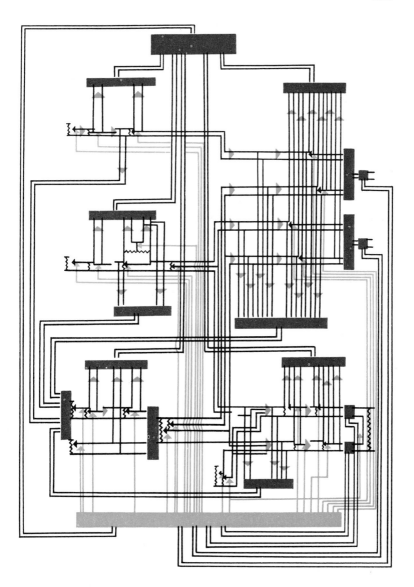

A possible electrical analogue of the interaction shown in the previous diagram. The places where decisions are required are traced in blue.

computer, with which the management would be able to play games—investigating the response of the system to various alternative stimuli. But the management concerned did not want the model in this physical form, and so the work proceeded on paper instead.

It was now possible to compute how one locality of the system would stabilize itself when perturbed by inputs from another locality. In fact, any large-scale mixed systems that is a going concern has features—call them intrinsic governors or decision-takers—that tend to make the total system self-regulating. If the managerial systems we create were not basically self-regulating, we should never be able to manage them; they would generate too much complexity for us to cope with. And so operational research identified precisely what was self-regulating about this system, using the servo model. It told us, by default, what was *not* self-regulating: That is to say, where managerial decisions had to be taken, on what evidence, and to what effect. The box marked " decisions " running along the bottom of the circuit diagram will not work unless it is given all the inputs shown. And the system as a whole cannot realize its maximum profitability unless all the decisions indicated are taken and are communicated to the places shown. Hence the research has now identified what information is needed to run the business, and how it has to be deployed.

A little reflection may suggest that this knowledge is itself extremely important, and rather hard to come by. Few businesses know these truths about themselves. But of course we wish to go further than this. A computable model of decision is required that will mix all the possibilities that now remain to be mixed, and arrive at optimal decisions. At last we have reached the final resolution and the final model in the hierarchy. We have come down the cone of resolution to the stage where answers to the problem can be obtained. Certainly, we have from moment to moment gone further than this, and made empirical investigations on the shop-floor and in the market about obscure areas of unresolved boxes. Then this information has gone up the cone of resolution again to help quantify the models at their various stages. Everything is now concentrated on the box labeled " decisions," and we are ready to use linear programming, as described.

Using Techniques to Answer Real-Life Questions

To get to this point, we have explored the cones of resolution, and created an interlocked hierarchy of models, each mapping onto its sucessor, each seeking to perform a different function in the chain. There were two conceptual models from ecology, supported by empirical investigation to ensure that the best way of discussing environmental dimensions was found. Then there was the move to make these conceptual models rigorous in a formulation from general systems theory, a mapping of these stochastic interactions onto a rigorous model from servomechanics, and then a final mapping of the relevant decision-taking elements onto a mathematical program. This means that the final mathematical and computational activity that gives the answer is actually *about* the real-life situation, and is not just an abstract theory about the way the business ought to be working.

Now the mixture of products and the interacting activity of the plant were examined together, under an optimizing functional set to maximize profit. It was discovered just where to make investments that would unlock the total system. Every local request for capital within the company was, as every accountant would expect, accompanied by a watertight " story " explaining why the investment would yield precisely that return on capital regarded as necessary by the company's board. But to reach a rational decision among these competing claims, we had to reevaluate the behavior of the entire ecological system assuming that each change had been made. It is not enough to examine the alleged benefits in the immediate locality of the investment, because of the reverberations the change will make throughout the system. It is the total profitability of the enterprise with which the management has to be concerned.

As we said before, a small local investment can so facilitate the overall behavior of the system that it ought to be selected for this reason. The new level of profit of the company at large absolutely attributable to this change can easily involve a return of several hundred per cent per annum on the capital that has to be invested. This is precisely because other assets than those freshly instituted are enabled to achieve their full potential by the money to be spent on this small investment.

When Reducing Costs Looked Too Costly

Although this case history did involve the whole enterprise, and cut across all the divisions of management, it was founded in a production situation. In particular, the market boxes in the ecological model were never very far resolved, because the management considered that they had the answers they needed. So the second case history to be quoted, which again involves the whole enterprise and again cuts across managerial boundaries, is chosen to illustrate the resolution of a marketing situation.

As before, and as so often happens, however, the problem did not arise in this form. The initial question was extremely interesting. It was necessary to build a new factory (one of several) and there was no gainsaying that fact, for one of the factories was literally falling down. Perhaps the new factory could be built on the same site, although this project posed difficulties, because production had to be maintained meanwhile. It might be a good idea to go somewhere else, thought the management. Where?

They found, however, that wherever they tried to site an alternative new factory, all advantage seemed likely to be lost in increased distribution costs.

Perhaps you would like to pause here to ask how this could possibly happen. The fact puzzled the management itself. But enough has been said in this book to indicate what the answer is. Remembering that we are dealing with a system in which a number of factories spread about the country is producing a consumer product to be retailed at all points—wherever there is a city, a town, or a village of adequate size. hence there is a stochastic network of distribution, of the kind we learned to expect earlier. There are subsidiary plants to the major factories; there are also warehouses and depots scattered about the countryside.

Well, management has created this elaborate network for retailing its products, and it has done so in the knowledge of where its factories are. Since it is a good management, it has done this sensibly and economically. Consequently, we are now faced with another of those systems that have a total identity that means more than the sum of the parts. This system is more than a distribution network that happens to distribute; it is a *machine for distributing*. And it is not just for distributing the product from anywhere to anywhere, but for distributing the product from particular places to other particular places. Its integrity as a system depends upon these particularities. Therefore, if we seek arbitrarily to change the location of a major factory, we destroy that machine's identity and integrity. We are trying to use the machine for a quite different purpose; and it is naïve to imagine that it will do a different job from the one it has evolved to do. The trouble is, of course, that people do not think of distribution arrangements as a vast machine having very special behavioral characteristics of its own. It is hard to think of it as if it were. But this is the only way.

Getting Past The Paradox to The Problem

I shall now ask you to take the difficult conceptual step of regarding what have hitherto been twin cones of resolution as superimposed. There is nothing special about having two cones —one could have any number. And perhaps the best generalization of the whole idea is in a single cone, in which everything is as integral as the general theory of systems demands that it should be. Now the model at the apex of this cone is simply a point labeled " the distribution system," which is defined as that machinery (in the invisible sense) that uncouples supply and demand. So this point tells us nothing at all. If we begin to descend the cone of resolution, the first level we reach involves the *logic* of the system.

We know that we are dealing with a network, and the first problem is to obtain some insight into the directionality of that network, and the regulations that govern it. The descriptive process here is certainly logical, because we are not so much concerned with financial or geographical factors as with the principles of the whole business. If we are not careful, we shall find that we are indifferently discussing flows of material from retailer to producer, as well as those the other way round—which are the ones that are important. Or we shall find that we admit the possibility that the entire content of the factory at a given time may go to one retail outlet. There is, however, *structure* in this system.

The first step, then, is to use general systems theory to obtain some resolution that has to do not with places and with costs but with logic. We shall write down, in rigorous form, the relationship between factories, subsidiary plants, warehouses, depots, and retail outlets—without saying how many there are of each. This means that from this point we are talking sense about distribution, without binding ourselves to any particular set of circumstances. We have created a distribution language, that, because it is logically rigorous, can be taught to a computer.

Now the next stage in resolution is to look at the geography of the country, in order to observe what the real terrain is like, for the unstructured network given in the first model will have to be stretched over the land if we are ever to decide on actual sites. The question is, then, how to obtain a rigorous representation of terrain. Fortunately there are large-scale maps that bear a grid system. Using a grid reference, it is possible to demarcate any actual point on the terrain to whatever degree of accuracy we like. Moreover, we are not concerned with *all* the features of this terrain. The only things that matter are the channels of distribution, namely roads and railroads. Here is a beautiful example of a homomorphic model. We need to map real terrain onto a numerical representation of it that preserves the structure of certain pathways and nothing else. This is readily done, given that we are going to use a computer. For there is a finite number of railways, and a finite number of roads capable of carrying heavy traffic. All that is necessary is to create a topographic model that contains this information.

The problem has now been resolved, through the use of two models, to the point where an abstract logical structure can be stretched over an actual terrain, all the details of both having been written down in a rigorous way the computer can accept. The next stage of resolution of the O.R. activity down the cone of resolution helps. For just as it proved unnecessary to produce a model of *every* feature of the geographic terrain, so it is unnecessary to map every aspect of cost. The focusing of the original logical model onto the terrain showed us what aspects of the terrain were important and ought to be modeled. So now some further resolution shows which costs are invariant (and can be forgotten) and which are dependent on the network under construction. These are the ones to resolve.

To do so, we need a model from the science of econometrics, which deals with the mathematical structure of economic relationships. This model, in the case being quoted, was of the following

135

form. We have to move goods from *A* to *B* (without knowing where these two places are). We know how far a truck can travel on roads in a day, depending on the classification of the terrain and on the rules applied by the trade unions to such duties. We can refer to the mileage involved as A – B, because we already have a topographic model that will select the route between these two points, rather than assuming a straight line between the two. (For obviously we cannot have trucks attempting to swim across unbridged estuaries, nor yet charging over precipitous mountains.)

We divide this A – B mileage by the relevant speed of transport, thereby obtaining the number of hours' traveling involved. This result then has to be partitioned by the regulations governing the working day. To it must be added the turn-round times of the lorries. You will see how we are building up a general formula for the time taken to go from any one point to any other, and of course this represents a cost. Part of this cost is taken up by wages, which we know about, and part by the value of the vehicle involved. We know what this is, too, and we incorporate the share of capital cost attributable to the journey.

To sum up: There are three hierarchically arranged models so far in the cone of resolution. The structural model has to be stretched over the topographical model, according to quantification principles introduced by the econometric model. Each stage makes the argument less general and more particular, and it chooses the particularity of the succeeding stage by focusing on what matters at the lower level. The whole thing may be represented inside a computer, because it is all described in rigorous terms. But are we now supposed to simulate all this, or to do mathematical programming on it, or what?

Consider the facts. We know how many factories there are at the moment, but do not know where all of them are—because one at least may have to be moved. Furthermore, if the company management is rightly disposed toward its use of management science, it may be (as it was in this case) ready to consider any recommendation that there should be more or fewer than this number of factories. It follows then, by even stronger arguments, that the present location of other links (warehouses, depots) in the distribution chain is subject to review, as is their number. In fact, the only thing we really know is the number and location of retail outlets. These are apparently satisfactory, but the first step is to do some checking upon the future of demand to see whether the location of the ultimate markets is likely to shift much over (say) the next twenty years. After this has been done (and it was done in this case) the problem takes on the following form.

Given a knowledge of the number and location of retail outlets, what is the best arrangement of production facilities *coupled with* distribution network to supply this market most economically? In considering this problem it is no use ignoring where the present sites of everything are, even though it has been agreed that these sites may be changed. For each factory and each depot represents a capital investment, and it has a certain outstanding value. Therefore any proposed move must take account not only of the cost of establishing a new location, but of the loss associated with abandoning the old.

Here then is the interesting point. We want a method for searching the country for all these facilities so as to choose the best collection. It is impossible to list and inspect all the potential sites, because they are infinite in number and the list could therefore never be completed. How *does* one choose between an infinite number of alternatives, to find the best?

Getting Past The Problem to The Solution

The way in which this problem was solved cannot be expounded in all its scientific ingenuity without a great deal of mathematics, and by assuming a considerable knowledge of computer technology. So the account given here is a little bit fanciful. It attempts to convey, in ordinary English, what the scientific strategy was all about. You will have to take my word for it that, if you can follow through the steps outlined, you will obtain a correct *feeling* for what was actually done.

We nominate someone to stand at each of the retail outlets, armed with the figures indicating the amount of supplies he has to obtain. This is the only place to start because this is the only piece of factual evidence we have. But each of these people stands on a peculiar map of our invention, and not on the actual terrain. The first thing about this peculiar map is that it stops his looking for a

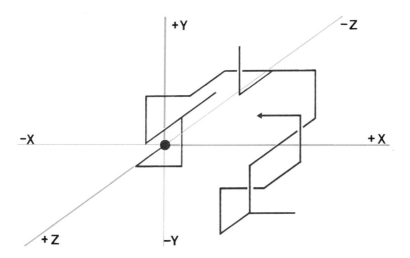

A computer-generated " random walk " in three dimensions. After each step the computer chooses the next step (+x, −x, +y etc.) at random. The " stubs " on the path show where a particular step (in one case, a series of two steps) was reversed on the next step. The possible consequences of quite complex situations can be explored with computers, using this technique.

factory before he has found a depot—and so forth. The constraints on his movement to achieve this are supplied by the logic of the structural model. The second thing is that he will find he can move only along established transportation routes, as determined by the topographic model, at rates established by the econometric model. Finally, he will find that he has to move up hills and down valleys that are quite unfamiliar.

These mountainous characteristics of his terrain are not at all those of the countryside with which he is familiar. They are supplied from the econometric model. The *height* of any point is given by the cost associated with that point for distribution purposes. So the object of each of the people involved in this experiment will be to move toward a depot, and thereafter to somewhere else (perhaps a warehouse, or a subsidiary plant, or to a factory direct), knowing the rule that the correct location of this place is the *lowest* point he can find.

So far so good. But if you imagine yourself as one of these people involved in the search, you will quickly perceive a snag. You are moving over a terrain of hills and valleys in search of the lowest point; *but so are your many colleagues.* These are the searchers who set out from other retail points, remember. And of course as your colleagues in this hunt move about on their particular searches, they will alter the costs associated with your search. Therefore your terrain changes its contours as you walk across it, and you cannot see ahead. The idea that you cannot see ahead is introduced to reflect the fact that you do not know how the terrain will change in the next few minutes, because there is no knowing what the other searchers will be up to. Therefore the problem confronting you is to find the lowest point, on a shifting terrain, in an obliterating fog.

Daunting though this exercise sounds, there is a simple strategy that you can follow. You stand still on one foot, and feel around you with the other foot until you find a point that is lower than the point on which you are already standing. You move to this point and repeat the process. By employing this strategy, then despite the shifting terrain, all the searchers will eventually find that they have reached the lowest point in their respective zones. The collection of these points is the correct answer to the management problem. The number of depots, warehouses, factories, and so on that are needed will be discovered too, because some of us will find ourselves standing on the same point. This happens when several outlets ought to be served from the same depot or factory.

I think the imagination boggles at only one aspect of this illustration: It might be that one of us will be standing in a local basin, unaware that there is a deeper valley just beyond. This is a limitation of the picture I have created, and not of the scientific model itself. For the picture assumes a three-dimensional space, in which local basins might obviously exist, whereas the actual model is multidimensional, and does not contain these land traps. It is quite possible (please believe) to arrange the logic of a search system of this kind so that there is always an exit from an apparent lowest point that leads to the genuine lowest point.

That is how the modeling was done. Now you may think that the task of computing the answer is too big, and that it would take too long ever to reach a practical conclusion; but again I have to remind you of the speed of modern computers. For we did not actually use people in this searching exercise; we did the job in a single day on one of the largest computers in the world. It took seventy experiments to resolve the issue. (You may envisage that as involving seventy halts in the search proceedings for the re-briefing of all concerned.) In each of these seventy experiments, all three models in the hierarchy (each one imposed and focused on the one below it) had to be evaluated a huge number of times. Many of the experiments meant that each had to be evaluated as many as a quarter of a million times. You probably realize that there is enough computation going on here to succeed in getting the right answer.

As a result of this job, with its hierarchy of models, the management found out where to site not only the one new factory, but *all* their production and distribution facilities. The report showed which existing facilities ought to be abandoned, and which new ones ought to be abandoned, and which new ones ought to be created—allowing for the costs and losses involved. And so a new distribution machine emerged. It allowed for the construction of a new factory, and said where it ought to be—which was the original question. But this time, the large savings attributable to a new production technology were preserved instead of being dissipated in increased distribution charges. Indeed, an equivalent sum in savings was able to be realized in terms of the distribution network itself. So instead of making x and then losing more than x, which was the original situation, the management learned of a new strategy that would enable it to increase its total profits by $2x$.

Secondly, we have to remember the point about the model as a growth asset. This company was contemplating further investments. It had thoughts of buying out competition, and of extending its markets. Obviously these prospects could be tested on the model already established, and the influence of various acquisitions on the proposed new distribution network could be ascertained.

At the end of World War II, when we first took operational research out of the military context and into industry, we used to define it quite simply as: Finding a quantitative basis for decision. We dropped that definition because people thought it meant simply finding the facts. It does mean finding the facts; but we might all be a little worried about that " simply."

6 The Viable Governor

It is clear from these stories that senior management grapples with some very large systems indeed. Some of the ways in which modern science has been able to aid the manager in formulating policies and in taking decisions have already been described. But, as was said at the outset, the manager's task is not restricted to those glamorous moments when he is occupied in one of these two tasks. The moment of decision may be dated and timed on a clock; important decisions are infrequent. The formulation of a policy may take much longer; but the process occupies a fairly well defined epoch. Much more important, because it is continuous and sustained, is the manager's function of *control*.

Much that has already been said bears on this matter, but the time has come to consider it more thoroughly. This does not mean, as many people imagine, embarking on a course of accountancy and the economics of the firm. Money in the form of capital assets may well provide the anatomy of a business, and liquidity—the flow of cash—is its lifeblood. It is hardly possible to overrate the

The development of the Watt governor for steam engines, which adapted the power output of the engine automatically to the load by means of feedback, consolidated the first Industrial Revolution.

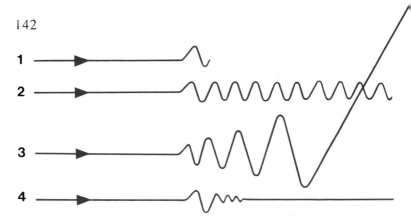

A disturbance in a system's output (1) may have different consequences according to the system. In (2) the system has gone into continuous oscillation. In (3) the oscillations grow until the system is destroyed. In (4) the oscillations disappear.

Instability in a mechanical system. The Tacoma Narrows Bridge was unstable in certain wind conditions, and oscillations that increased in amplitude finally destroyed the " system."

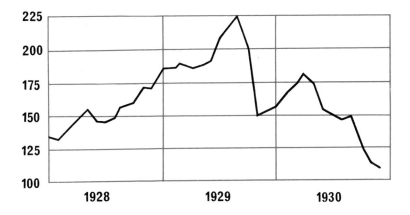

Instability in an economic system is shown by this record of stock prices on the New York Stock Exchange during the years 1927–1930. Note that the final collapse was preceded by periods of increasing instability.

importance of financial control for these reasons. But it would be an equal and opposite, though extremely common, mistake to imagine that financial control and the leadership of men exhausts the control functions of management.

What do we mean when we say that a system is " in control?" There are several important marks. Firstly, the output of the system (or the output that happens to be of interest to us) is held steady. We tend to watch this in practice by watching what happens to output if the system is disturbed in its peaceful running. Inevitably, the output is disturbed as well: but if the system is in control, the oscillation damps down. The best word for " being in control " in this sense is *stability*. If a system is unstable, then the disturbance of its smooth running may lead to violent oscillations in the output, which increase in magnitude after the cause of the disturbance has been withdrawn.

Secondly, we expect systems that are in control to maintain this kind of stability without our needing to take exceptional or panic measures to achieve the result. Constant surveillance and intervention ought not to be necessary.

It is easy enough to test an engineering system for these two properties, but not so easy to detect them in an industrial, social, or economic system. We may not be able to identify the inputs and outputs of such systems in an unambiguous fashion—and this may stop us from using a clear-cut model from servomechanics (as we did in Chapter 5). Moreover, we may be able to determine what counts as exceptional action within a system of this kind, and this will preclude our making any sort of measure of its degree of self-regulation.

So, and thirdly, we tend to judge whether such a system is in control by assessing its internal coherence, the smoothness of its operation. This also is a subjective judgment, but it turns out to have serious implications. The point is this: If people use this indirect criterion of smoothness as evidence of being in control, they may come to regard smoothness instead of in-control-ness as the object of the exercise, *and this will make them resistant to change.*

It thus becomes important to find ways of talking sensibly about the nature of control in large systems. This is the function of the science of cybernetics, of which mention has been made previously. But whereas in Chapter 3 we were concerned to take a model from this science, we are now contemplating a more basic issue. For if cybernetics is the science of control, and if management might be described as the profession of control, there ought to be a topic called *management cybernetics*—and indeed there is. It is the activity that applies the findings of fundamental cybernetics to the domain of management control.

Implicit Control

All books that talk about self-regulating systems begin their formal analysis with a description of the Watt steam governor. This is an early, and very beautiful, example of a self-regulating device; so even if it bores you to see the picture of it, I feel I should be letting you down if it were not included. Besides, I want to make a most important point about this device, which may not have occurred to you before. First of all, just check on your understanding of how the thing works. If the engine turns too quickly, the balls fly outward due to increased centrifugal force.

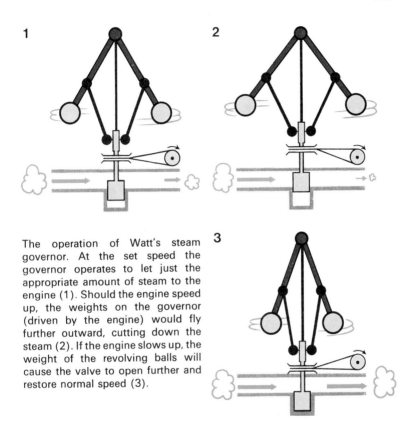

The operation of Watt's steam governor. At the set speed the governor operates to let just the appropriate amount of steam to the engine (1). Should the engine speed up, the weights on the governor (driven by the engine) would fly further outward, cutting down the steam (2). If the engine slows up, the weight of the revolving balls will cause the valve to open further and restore normal speed (3).

This has the effect of turning a valve that reduces the supply of steam to the engine, so that it returns to the preselected speed. If the engine slows below the desired speed (due to an increased load, perhaps) the balls move inward, the valve opens further, more steam is admitted, and the engine picks up speed again. Thus the system regulates itself, and its output is called *stable* for the reasons given above.

The feature that I want to hammer home is this. Controllability is *implicit* in the operation of the machine. Let me quote my favorite example to explain what this is supposed to mean. Consider a prison. This is a closed system containing a number of variables—called convicts. What is the output of this system? For purposes of this example, I want to say that the system has no output. The convicts are supposed to be locked up inside; if one of the variables runs away, then the system is out of control. Suppose that as we observe this system a convict does escape. There is eventually a roll call at which his absence is discovered, and then we observe the system ringing bells, sending out search parties, and taking all sorts of action to bring the variable back into control. This system is certainly self-regulating in some sense.

It happens that this prison is, like the steam engine, controlled by a Governor. His method of controlling involves inspecting all the variables from time to time to see that they are all in control. If his inspection system eventually reveals that one of them has gone out of control, a train of events is started by which the escaper may (or may not) be recaptured. The interesting thing is that this control system may not work—it may be defeated. Control may break down because there are inherent weaknesses in the system, in particular the lags between successive inspections of the prisoners. So the prison governor may be taking dinner with his guests while his charges are tunneling their way under the walls.

The problem with managing either a business or a prison by periodic rather than continuous inspection is that the " variables " are likely to be seriously out of control before the discrepancy is noted.

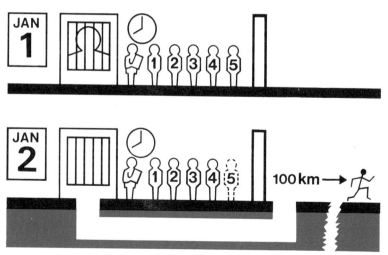

The steam governor, on the contrary, does not rely on separated inspections, nor does it initiate a series of events any one of which may go wrong, nor does it include several time lags of which escaping variables may take advantage. It is an implicit controller: Variables are brought back into control *in the act of and by the act of* going out of control. It is as if every convict were chained to the prison by an invisible piece of elastic that would pull him back to his cell—whether anybody saw him leave it or not, whether the alarm system worked or not, whether the posse of warders found him or not.

There is a difference between a self-regulating system that one confidently expects to go right, and a self-regulating system that cannot go wrong. Management, I fear, almost always uses the first. It ought to be the second. You will recall the excellent principle " management by exception." This says that everything that matters in the management domain should be compared with a norm. Only those events that are exceptions to the normal rule will be brought to managerial attention. This is, it seems to me, a way of trying to express the need for implicit control, because the idea is that a variable going out of control should advertise the fact rather than wait until a routine managerial inspection identifies the fact. But this is not enough.

Governors, or implicit controllers, depend for their success on two vital tricks. The first is *continuous and automatic* comparison of some behavioral characteristic of the system against a standard. The second is a *continuous and automatic* feedback of corrective action. Management is certainly aware of both tricks, and makes considerable effort to employ them. But it does not normally achieve continuous monitoring, nor automatic corrective action. This is not so much because it is difficult to do either of these things, but because the model of the governor is not used. In other words, managerial experience has discovered what sort of thing to do (of course it has), but it has not necessarily found the best way of doing it.

Let us look at a production control system that depends on machine loading. This is not quite as specialized a topic as might at first appear; that is to say, it is not simply the province of the works manager. For what the works believes to be its experience of

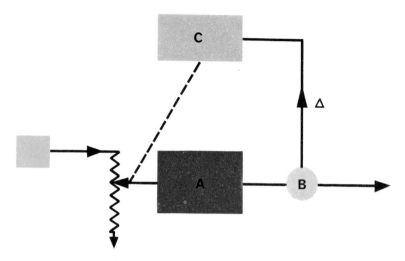

The general feedback loop. The output of A is compared against the desired standard at B, the difference (Δ) is fed to C, which adjusts the input to A until Δ ≅ O, within the limits required.

smoothness in production flow turns out to determine most features of the company's operating policy. Tenders made to customers will depend on beliefs as to price and delivery date, and indeed these will decide whether the tender is made at all. Costs will vary with (for instance) the times allocated to machine-jobs on the plant. The satisfaction of the customer, in terms of price and delivery at least, will be affected too. And so on. Why do I say " beliefs "? Surely the times and costs allocated to the production of goods are susceptible to objective measurement, and surely—even if these measurements are sometimes wrong—they are still measurements rather than beliefs? Unfortunately not.

You may remember how in Chapter 2 we discussed the " variety " of a system that has to be controlled. We worked out that a manager controlling ten processes might have to consider ten million production plans. In fact, the variety of any real-life production control system is far too great to permit the objective measurement in detail of all the possible states of affairs that might

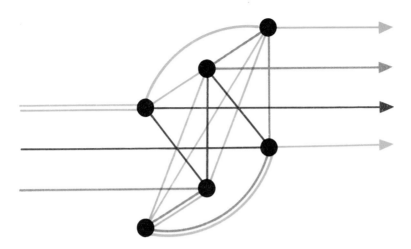

The difficulty of managing " by exception." The diagram shows the path of
four orders among six machines or processing steps in a jobbing plant.
The route of each order is determined by the particular requirements of that
order; there are 720 possible orders in which all six machines could be used.

exist. What we do, even in a works that has been exhaustively time-
studied is to group possibilities together, to average out results over
such groups, and to fill in the blanks with "guesstimates." And
even while we are in the act of investigating this amount of insight,
the situation is surreptitiously changing. According to one of the
key laws of cybernetics, which was also invoked earlier in this book,
the variety of the controller must be at least as great as the variety
of the situation to be controlled, and this requirement is likely to
be falsified. It can be met in a mass production situation: But as
the production possibilities fan out, it becomes less and less
possible. In a typical jobbing works, the task is hopeless.

This is why "management by exception" has not really fulfilled
its promise. It is based on the right idea, but in practice it becomes
impossible to detect what really is an exception, until it is too late.
When the exception is detected, after a considerable postmortem, it
may well be discovered that there is no repeat order for this item
anyway. So the hard-won information is no use.

What Should be Controlled?

The way to use management cybernetics and the principle of intrinsic control in this situation is as follows. We should not try to measure the variable characteristics of every machine and every job and every machine-job. We should instead measure something rather more sophisticated—an output of our system that we expect to remain steady. Various choices are open. A statistic I have often used with success is the ratio of planned to actual time. This (you will note) is a pure number, applicable to every job regardless of the machines used or the nature of the product. It reduces variety straight away, therefore. Moreover, it invariably turns out that production as measured in these terms is more homogeneous than anyone has suspected. The statistical analysis of a population of ratios (as opposed to a population of heterogeneous jobs) is a simple and rewarding exercise.

Now if the job-recording system automatically computes the appropriate ratio, this can be routinely compared with the norm ratio for the product group to which the job belongs. In this way the first criterion of the governor principle is met; that is to say, there will be continuous and automatic comparison between what is and what should be the case. Secondly, the very next forecast made in this product group (as statistically defined) can be weighted by a factor that measures the statistical significance of the disagreement between that measure and the norm. And so the second criterion is met as well, for this is the continuous and automatic feedback we require.

A much more lengthy exposition of the technique involved is required than we have space to recount, before anyone could say: I will do this. But this is not a textbook. What matters is that we should understand the principles through which management may make new advances, and illustrate these principles through practical examples. The approach to production control briefly described here certainly works; moreover, the method has been used in other contexts (for instance, cost control) as well, with a very considerable degree of success. But we must return to the argument, which was about very large and very complicated situations.

Then you may reply: It is all very well to talk about a works and the problems of production control. However complicated this situation may be, there are at least identifiable machines, processes, and products; these can be inspected and measured. But we began by talking of systems more elaborate than this, systems in which most of the variables would not be measurable, or even identifiable. So we must now generalize the cybernetic thinking to take account of much more difficult situations. There is, for instance, the penological system; or there is a transportation network; or a system of docks; or (to return to the favorite case) there is the entire firm. How does one proceed in these cases, and what then happens to the principle of the governor, and to its tricks of comparison and feedback.

I must again refer you to the previous chapter, and the case where a hierarchy of models began with a simple ecological situation. Management has much to learn from the cybernetics of ecology, for a reason that (at this stage of the book) ought to be immediately appealing. The fact is that living systems—interacting animal populations—are intrinsically controlled. They are *viable* governors.

When one comes to think about it, most of our managerial philosophy is based on authority and its delegation. We normally seek to control situations of high variety by dividing them into subsystems we then set up sufficient sub-controllers to absorb the variety implicit in the situation. This is sound practice in cybernetic terms, but it is not the only nor the most economical approach to the job. What nature has to tell us about the problem is something very different.

By the criteria set out at the start of this chapter, nature is " in control." We know, for example, that there are myriads of insects and small beasts all around us, and we know that these proliferate at fantastic rates. And yet we never stop to ask ourselves how it is that we are not drowned in a sea of caterpillars, squeezed to death by frogs (just think of all that frog spawn), or pecked to death by birds. It is not an easy question to answer, even though one fully appreciates the basic device that nature uses—the device whereby things eat each other. Thinking strictly in managerial terms, it really is fantastic that the whole system works. Indeed, on the few occasions when something goes slightly wrong, we are moved more

Whether a system is in control depends on one's breadth of view. Natural systems maintain stability by a number of complexly interlocking food chains. To the moth in the picture above, the overall stability of the system is of only academic interest, however.

to annoyance than to wonder; we complain that there is a plague of ants, or that some blight has killed off our roses. But these rare exceptions should persuade us of the fantastic efficacy of the control system at large. There are no managers, no controllers, no sub-controllers, no bureaucracy, and no paper work, in an ecological control system. There is instead intrinsic control. A particular population tending to increase is *ipso facto* short of food and its breeding rate falls. It is the Watt steam governor all over again, but with this interesting difference. We have here a vast network of interacting governors. The network is so complicated that ecologists will rarely agree to the identification of any one on its own. They talk instead about food webs, and regard the very complexity of the system as its main stabilizing feature. By this I mean (to refer to the cybernetic argument in Chapter 3) that there is no unique feedback, no unsupported control loop, on which the whole system depends, And just because of this, the whole business is an excellent model of business itself.

Homeostasis and Ultrastability
The self-regulating properties of a system such as this were discovered by the cybernetician Ross Ashby. The name of the special kind of self-control that it exerts is *homeostasis*. Control in this case still depends on feedback, whereby some function of the output of one subsystem becomes part of the input of another subsystem. In fact there has to be a rich interaction between each of the subsystems and most of all the others (think again of the prey and predator situation in ecology). We have the basic mathematics that reveal how the whole thing works; but what concerns us here are two special properties of such an arrangement.

First of all, what does a homeostat actually do? The answer is that it holds the critical variables of the system stable within *physiological* limits. This means to say that the limits are fixed by the capacity of the whole organism to operate satisfactorily within them. Physiological limits are not arbitrarily imposed from outside, they are generated from within.

For example, the classic case of homeostasis is the control of blood temperature. As you know, one may move quickly from a refrigerator to the stage of a steel-melting shop: elaborate mechanisms in the body will adjust its temperature at all times closely to its norm of 37°c. Why 37°? Certainly not because some authority has said that this is right, but because the organism itself recognizes its own optimal working temperature. Similarly, the physiological limit is one that the system itself recognizes as dangerous to exceed. Thus 37°c is no more than a measure of centrality between upper and lower physiological limits. If we have seemed in the last few paragraphs to have wandered away from the subject of management, I hope it is now clear why the concept I have been developing is so important. We were arguing, remember, that real-life managerial situations are so complicated that it may not be possible to recognize or to nominate which are the critical outputs of the system, nor to specify the values to which those outputs ought to be held steady. Clearly, if it is possible to have a self-regulating system that *implicitly* arranges its own stability, then this is of the keenest management interest.

The second point about homeostasis is that it procures an especially valuable kind of equilibrium, which is known as *ultrastability*. This is a precisely defined mathematical concept, but I shall try to make its meaning clear in words.

You will recall that stability was explained in terms of disturbances to the system. When a smooth-running system is disturbed, its output is disturbed: a stable system quickly restores that output to its old value by damping down the oscillation produced. But of course when we were talking about straightforward feedback governors, we reckoned that we knew the type of disturbance we were talking about. One can design a servomechanism, just like a Watt governor, to deal with disturbances originating in a limited number of known and nominated inputs. No one would expect that controller to succeed in handling kinds of disturbances other than those that it was designed to handle. If, then, someone were to creep up on the system and shake it, no one would complain if it went out of control.

But in big managerial systems this is precisely the trouble. They are indeed shaken by all sorts of disturbances that we may not have thought about when we arranged the set of management controls. So we should like the homeostat to regain its equilibrium after it

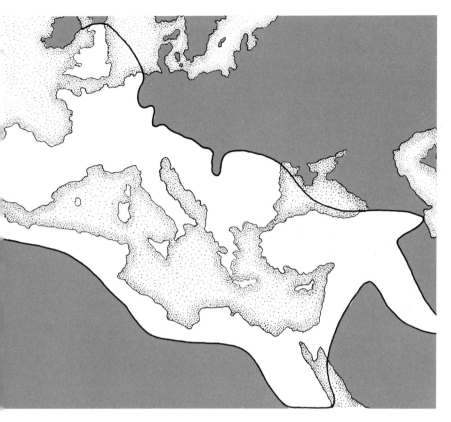

The Roman Empire, shown here at its height, was the most impressive management program in history. Its success was partly due to extensive use of indigenous homeostatic mechanisms by the Roman conquerors.

has been disturbed from *any* cause, even a cause not hitherto experienced at all. And that is what ultrastability is: a capacity in a system to regain equilibrium after any kind of perturbation, including kinds the designer did not have in mind. So once more we see that this sort of controllability is of great interest to management.

Although we have " always known " that natural systems, the ecological ones, exhibited both these highly desirable forms of self-regulation, we have taken them for granted. When they are laid here, the properties do sound rather magical. It may help to realize that the claims made for homeostasis are not boundless. If we return to the example of body temperature, it is clear that if we lock our subject in the refrigerator for a week, or actually throw him into the furnace, he will not survive. There is, in short, a threshold of disturbances beyond which the system is denatured, if not actually annihilated. This is like saying that even the Watt governor will not work if it is blown up, or if it falls apart. But these limiting situations do not rob homeostats of their importance and value. They achieve ultrastability within physiological limits for a range of behavior within environmental limits.

We must now make some attempt to understand how this surprising mechanism actually works. The example taken is artificially simplified, so that it is no more than a small extension of the ecological interaction we have already examined.

A New Model

Here is a new version of the old, simple diagram showing the interaction of an organism and its environment. We were thinking of them in Chapter 5, remember, as the Company and its market. The boxes representing these two things, which used to be blank because we said nothing about them, are now filled with dots. This

The red dots each represent a possible state of the whole firm (left) and market (right). If the firm forces the market into a non-preferred state (outside the circle) the market feedback will ask the firm to advise accordingly.

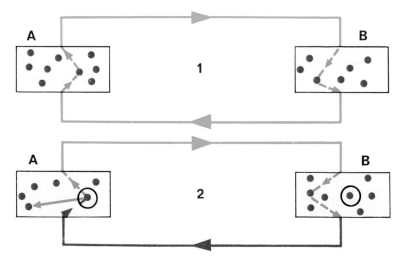

is so novel a departure in our mode of drawing diagrams in this book that I would ask you to consider rather carefully what it means. Each dot represents a possible state of the company or the market. There are of course many many millions of dots, and neither the company nor the market can be represented by more than one of them at any given moment. On this basis it is possible to complete the loop around the whole system by showing the trajectory followed from input to output in each subsystem. The dashed line is that trajectory: It is simply a way of pointing to the dot that represents the state of affairs " now."

It is obvious that some states are preferable to others. After all a whole lot of *possible* states of the company would eventually lead to bankruptcy; others, on the contrary, would lead to highly profitable outcomes. Let us, then, collect the most preferred dots together, and enclose them in a circle. It is now obvious that we wish the trajectory of control to select a dot within the circle rather than outside.

If this argument can be applied to the company, it can also be applied to the market. For instance, it might be immediately profitable to the company to make large quantities of a shoddy product. The control trajectory would then indicate a satisfactory state of affairs on the left-hand side of the diagram. But the shoddy product would evoke an unfavorable response in the market, which means that the second trajectory would indicate a dot that did not belong to the preferred set of market states. The argument is symmetrical. For it would be useless to attend to the market trajectory by (for example) producing an excellent product and selling it at less than cost, because this would quickly force the company's trajectory out of its preferred, profitable circle. We can now see how the system works. The company takes an action that satisfies its own criteria of success. This provokes a " message " around the uppermost loop and affects what is going on in the market, altering its trajectory. This change propagates a message around the lower loop to alter the state of affairs in the company. And so on. Homeostatic equilibrium is reached when what is happening in each subsystem results in the representative point of the other system being chosen from its preferred set of states. In that case, no action is required by anyone: The system goes on cycling quite happily to everybody's satisfaction. This is precisely the criterion of " smoothness " that we noticed much earlier. But if something happens to change the trajectory in one of the boxes so that the representative point is forced outside the circle, the governors inside that subsystem will operate to bring it back. This will produce a change in the messages reaching the other subsystem, and may force *its* representative point into a danger zone. The total system then begins to oscillate until both points, and not just one of them, have returned to safety. Ashby called this part of the mechanism " self-vetoing." Every time one of the subsystems achieves success, it effectively sends a message to the other saying: " I am all right." If the second subsystem is not satisfied by this input, it vetos that state of affairs by replying: " You may be all right but I am not: Do something else."

We spoke of the magical theorem of ultrastability which says that systems can be designed to be stable under *any* disturbance. As with all magic, it seems so easy once you know how the trick is done. For consider: This self-regulator recognizes the results of disturbance rather than the nature of disturbance, and takes action to avoid unpleasant consequences without attempting to resist their unknown causes. So if we jog the system in some totally unexpected way it will respond by seeking a new equilibrial state, and return to smooth behavior.

I am conscious that this account, being very much simplified, may seem an inadequate model of the complicated kind of management situation with which it will have to deal. In fact, it must in use be much more elaborately developed. The trouble is that one cannot depict the elaboration very successfully with diagrams alone, and this is no place for a mathematical treatment. You can also imagine that the verbal description of a system having, say, thirty subsystems (instead of two) all interacting, with each of these in turn having several equilibrial zones (instead of one), would be impossible either to write down or to follow. Yet the cybernetic models we use are such multiple, polystable homeostats.

However, our diagrams do go on to show something that looks a good deal more like the business situation with which management is concerned. In order to understand it, one must think of little homeostatic subsystems in every one of the boxes drawn, and of homeostatic supersystems that link the boxes together. If that effort of imagination can be made, the relevance of cybernetic theory to management practice may begin to be appreciated.

We have reached, after all, a stage where management ought to recognize the kind of cybernetic mechanism that underlies its routine way of operating. I do wish to make it abundantly clear in this context that the management scientist does not claim to make shattering new discoveries about the nature of business. He knows very well that the management understands its job. This repeats the philosophy outlined in Chapter 1, but it is worth repeating. All we are trying to do is to provide a rigorous account of what the manager knows, in order that his problems may be quantified, and answers computed rather than intuited. Let us take a case in point.

The annual budgetary appropriation made by a company for exploiting its market is (we might as well admit) a fairly arbitrary sum of money. This has to be divided (again by somewhat arbitrary means) between the various functions of marketing: advertising, distribution, packaging, market research, product research, and so on. In a big organization, each of these functions may well have its own management structure and organization, and be a separate activity in its own right. This undoubtedly means that there are homeostatic interactions within the very departments of the company's own marketing organization!

But the process of rather arbitrary division of the appropriation does not stop here. In advertising, for example, further breakdowns of the money available have to be made, as between various media; the press, television, hoarding displays, and so forth. Take any one of these divisions. In press advertising, for example, decisions will have to be taken as to how money should be divided between newspapers and journals, between full, half, and quarter pages. In the case of television, decisions will be needed about the frequency of occurrence, the timing of display, between thirty-second advertisements, and so on—until the money is spent. And what applies to the advertising branch applies to all the others.

This picture is entirely familiar to marketing men, just as an analogous picture of production would be familiar to the man in the works. The picture is indeed common to the whole of business, industrial and governmental management: a division of functions,

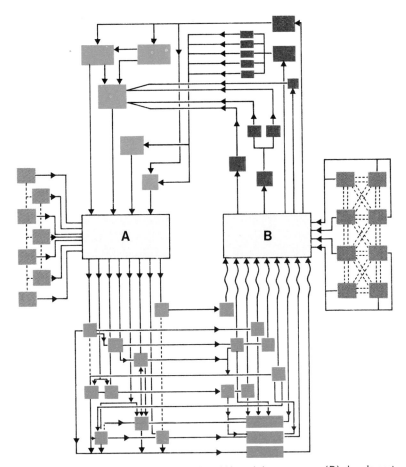

A model for the interaction of the market (A) and the company (B) developed in greater detail. The tan boxes represent competitors' activity; the brown boxes, random disturbances. The red boxes represent sales activities (research, advertising, special offers, etc.), the blue boxes customer characteristics (preferences, exposure to advertising, etc.); and green boxes represent actual purchasing behavior and its reporting to the company. The wavy lines suggest a certain distortion in the feedback to the company.

a division of staffs, a division of money. And the process of division is one that continues down from the single point of the total relevant appropriation, through a very large number of stages, to the great variety of separate bills that are eventually paid. It might, rather cynically, be said that it is only the fact that the total of these bills equals the original appropriation which provides any coherence in the marketing policy. For we must be realistic. In a big enterprise, all these subdivisions of which we have been speaking are small empires of ambitious men, and they are quite openly competing with each other.

Now each of these branches is trying to be responsible about its work. Most of them will be found making quite extensive use of scientific methods of one kind or another—particularly of forecasting techniques, for example. But what are we to say of the grand strategy itself? Most marketing men believe that the major decisions are matters of judgment and flair. But they are now invited to look at the question with new eyes.

The reason why the accepted policy relies on intuition is pretty clear. No one knows enough about the details of the boxes shown in the diagram to predict the total consequences of any change in any of the expenditures discussed. We cannot firmly identify all the inputs and all the outputs of the system; we certainly cannot specify the transformations effected in each of the little boxes; we do not know the physiological limits of any part of the system (except perhaps the one that measures our own liquid assets). We shall certainly try to experiment. For example, we may discontinue one kind of advertising in one part of the country, install a new kind in another part of the country, and then try to detect the difference in sales effectiveness. Sometimes these experiments work and reveal much. More often, they become totally confused by the action of competitors, and other arbitrary interferences.

The cybernetic model, by concentrating on the particular measures of homeostasis that matter to the company, such as the ultrastability of return on capital invested, overcomes many of these classic difficulties. Again, it has the great advantage possessed by all models, namely that one does not necessarily have to experiment with the actual situation. If sufficient data can be obtained to derive an (even rather rough) quantification of the homeostat, then experiments on its ultrastability can be run by simulation techniques. People often misdirect themselves by thinking that a simulation is no use unless every detail of the system has been measured. We saw why this is untrue in principle: Remember the argument from cones of resolution. Here we see the point, once again, in practice. For this simulation is not required in order to make specific quantified forecasts. Its job is to investigate stability, ultrastability, and the system's physiological limits.

Once again it is necessary to remind ourselves that we are trying to do some engineering with known effects rather than supposed causes, and with measures of tendency rather than absolute values. If it can be shown that a system of this kind is tending to build up a lopsided pressure on some part of a homeostat, then we may infer that the system will oscillate indefinitely unless something is done to correct this pressure. This is quite different from saying that a given policy will result in an increase in sales of x per cent. But in managerial terms it is even more useful, as well as being more honest. We have to face the fact that we cannot predict the future in detail. But our rigorous analysis can show that some loop of the control system is missing, that some of the laws known to govern systems of this kind are being disobeyed, or that some subsystems are placing undue stresses on others.

The Education of Systems

Let us now go back to the main thread of the argument to pick up a final and major thought. We were surely right to think of viable governors as seeking, first and foremost, stability. An unstable organism, after all, is likely to go out of existence, or to go mad; our very first task, as men or as companies, is to survive. But the arguments we have so far examined may well have provoked the uncomfortable feeling that we are making too great a virtue of staying safely in the same place. What do we mean by progress, if any deviation from smooth performance is to be cut back?

The answer to this question is directly obtainable from cybernetic theory, derived from a study of living systems. We do expect such systems (our children, for example, if not ourselves) to improve their performance on the basis of experience—that is to say, we expect them to *learn*. If the circumstances surrounding the system should radically change, then we expect the system to *adapt* to its new environment. Finally, as time passes, we normally find that the system *grows* and *evolves*. Learning and adaptation, growth and evolution, are really implicit in the concept of survival, even though its precondition may be a static-seeming ultrastability.

It is in fact not difficult to see how viable governors cause the systems in which they are implicit to learn. A simple-minded definition of learning is to say that the time taken to reach a stable response to a given stimulus shortens as the stimulus is repeated. Now we know that a particular set of circumstances may provoke a disturbance in a homeostatic system which throws the representative point of that system onto a new trajectory. We also know that the oscillations of the homeostat will not cease until this aberrant behavior has been restored to a successful outcome. Given that the subsystem is indeed made up of a host of interacting factors, which include the personalities of many human beings, it is not surprising to find that the path taken by the trajectory itself in restoring the status quo is facilitated as time goes by. In ordinary words, everyone finds out what to do. Individuals are certainly learning; much more importantly, the system as a whole is learning too.

If there is a real change in the environment, then the adaption required to meet this change is really a special kind of learning, which will involve some restructuring of the system itself. But of course the basic homeostatic mechanism is perfectly capable of resolving this problem. To do so, it may have to set up new sets of preferred states, which are more survival-worthy than the old, and to see how this may happen we shall have to envisage new loops in the total system that record and feed back types of information not considered in our original explanation. But in practice this is not difficult to achieve.

In particular, we may replace the simple circle that defined the set of preferred states with a kind of contour map of concentric circles. This takes our diagram into a third dimension, in which the representative states of subsystems are registered on a " height " scale denoting payoff. Then it will be a function of the system not only to procure a trajectory taking the representative point into the circle, but to climb the hill inside the circle too. This concept embeds a well-known operational research technique within the

To be really useful, computers, like any other tools, must be of a size suited to the requirements of the particular user.

The very active and complex interactions within a commodity exchange, such as the Chicago Board of Trade (Corn Exchange), allow a high degree of stability in the very complex cereal demand and supply system to be achieved.

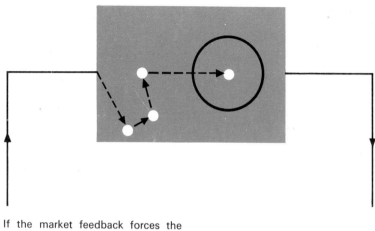

If the market feedback forces the
company into an unsatisfactory
state, internal adjustments within the
company must be made to restore
the trajectory to one passing through
the preferred circle again.

cybernetic theory, and presents no difficulty to the scientist. Hence the whole theory of viable governors can be taken as far as we wish to go. It is already proving immensely useful in practice. But this is worth stating: We are dealing here with a scientific method of inquiry into a particularly difficult zone, the domain of board-level judgment (often value judgment at that). We are not dealing with a technique of which one can say: We used it, and it repaid its cost in a year. The purpose of management cybernetics is, to this extent, rather different from the purpose of operational research. The cybernetician is seeking better control structures for the firm. When he obtains them, there is no doubt that the firm benefits. But the payoff is in terms of goodwill (for better deliveries), of increased metabolism (for higher productivity and sales effectiveness), of sounder long-range policy (in consequence of deeper insights into the mechanism of business). One cannot readily put a price on this head.

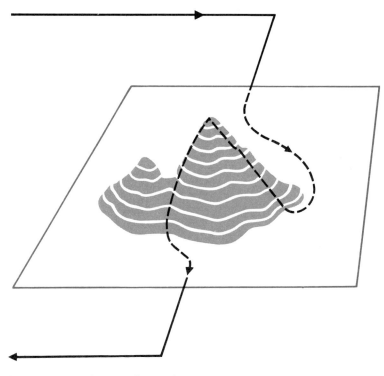

The company, of course, has an internal criterion—maximizing profits —on which it selects a satisfactory state, as well as attending to the feedback from the market. The usual problem is that the market feedback does not permit a path that reaches the summit of the company's profit hill.

7 Automation and Such

Most of the actual operational research studies discussed in this book have made use of the electronic computer. Is the work of management science *really* a question of making computer applications in industry, then? People could be forgiven for thinking so, and some do. But the viewpoint is nonetheless quite wrong. As was said at the start, the move toward scientific management has been going on throughout the century, and we have had operational research under that name since 1938. If the whole thing really depends on computers, what were we doing until the 1950s, when these machines first became commercially available?

No, the right answer to this question is that every kind of science in every epoch tends to deploy the tools of science available at the time. The mathematical backing of the differential calculus is nowadays routinely available in science: It is taken for granted. Yet science existed before Newton and Leibniz, who invented this tool, were born. Even today, plenty of scientific work goes on—e.g. in biology—that does not avail itself of this well-tried aid.

One of the ancestors of the modern sequence-controlled computer was the Jacquard Loom, in which the complex pattern of the weaving is controlled by a series of punched cards, the first-known application of this technique.

It is the same with computers. One uses them or not, depending on the need. (Beware of the mania which declares that science without computers is not science.) But if we stop to think about it at all, we can see that the management task concerns very complicated situations. Indeed, if the arguments of this book are correct, they are even more complicated than management itself believes. So we take computers for granted. In particular, we have championed the view that management science ought not to be confined by the conventional divisions of management: It ought to cut across them. The systems that make up the enterprise and that science knows how to describe are bigger and more complex than their stereotyped parts. So it is extremely *natural* that the management scientist should use the modern scientific tool that most particularly makes elaborate computation possible for very large systems; it is *not* a prerequisite.

Now what is true for the scientist is true for the manager himself. The profession of management has increasingly commanded scientific tools from which to fabricate an industrial technology and a managerial control apparatus. The first industrial revolution mechanized muscle power: It gave us ways of lifting, pushing, and pulling that were independent of human effort. Moreover, in support of mechanized effort it gave us mechanized precision and tolerances that the human hand could not achieve.

As time advanced, we entered an era of advanced mechanization. This made *sequences* of operations automatic. It gave to industry not only muscle power and precision skills by the push of a button, but controlling operations too. The self-positioning operations of a turret lathe, and the capability of a transfer line to move pieces of work from one set of operations to another—all these removed the need for human intervention in control.

Industry and Evolution

Let us use a conceptual model from physiology to describe how the situation developed. Before the Industrial Revolution, industry had grown itself a body with a workable anatomy. But it was not energized, and could be made to work only by using men, women, and children to pull on the tendons and to pump the blood. Mechanization introduced the energetics. Low energy messages

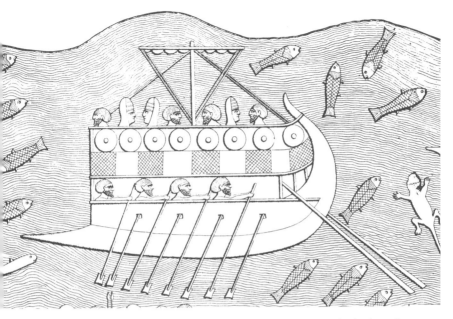

The earliest stages of mechanization involved the quite direct substitution of power machinery for human muscle, as shown in the design of Fitch's early steamboat compared to the muscle-driven Assyrian boat above.

Two steps in automation. In the turret lathe above, a number of premounted tools are sequentially brought into play. In the 14-station-in-line transfer machine below, several operations may be performed at each station (as in the turret lathe) but also the work-piece (here an automobile cylinder block) is automatically passed to the next station with no intervening handling.

were used to trigger off high-powered operations—to contract the muscles and to feed the system at large. With advanced mechanization, the body acquired nervous control up to the level of reflex. The body was innervated, and had acquired a spinal cord.

The most involved, and in general clever, applications of mechanization of this day are so adroit that they command our admiration and amazement. This is so much the case that we are invited to use the latest prestige word, *automation*, to describe them; but the tendency to do so should be resisted. For automation means more than this. Although inevitably a part of the evolution of man's mastery over the tasks of making things and providing services, it is novel to this extent: It provides an automatic counterpart of decision. There *is* something novel here, and we ought to see clearly what it is.

To continue with the physiological model, automation adds to mechanization the computational abilities of a brain. It means providing a facility to make a choice. And, like a brain, automation can fulfill this task only if it is provided with criteria of success. There is no need to think of automation, or of brains, as terribly mysterious in this respect. Given the incoming data, and given the criteria, automative machinery (whether in a metal box or in the skull) can undertake to choose. Operational research itself has uncovered the mechanism of choice. So this is the mark of automation we should seek: automatic decision-taking capacity. Because it is a prestige word, automation is used as a marketing slogan by some people who are really selling advanced mechanization, and who should (and probably do) know better. Always look for the telltale mark: a rudimentary capacity to decide. It is this that heralds the second industrial revolution.

The physiological model we are using gives us one more clue, this time about the future. We ourselves show a capacity to decide, which in many respects is programmed into us. What we think of as a human prerogative, and a special creative capability, is very largely neither of these things. For the teaching we receive as we grow up programs our brains for decisions. Yet there certainly is somewhere in us a greater capacity of decision—namely, to decide on the *basis* of decision, to specify our own criteria of success.

It is no use expostulating in a self-indulgent panic that we ourselves are more than living machines. Perhaps, indeed, we are. (I think so, if it is of any interest.) But it pays to bear in mind that, whatever our ultimate nature as individuals, what we *do* is mediated through the machinery of the brain. And cybernetics increasingly discovers how the brain works these tricks. Once the way one of these tricks works is known and can be formally specified, there is no real problem in designing man-made machinery that can do the trick as well. So it is not impossible to envisage an automated company of the future that is capable of formulating its own policy. Today we know how to take decisions automatically; this new facility—proposing a third industrial revolution on the horizon—would specify the framework of decision. And this phase in mankind's evolution has already been called *cybernation*.

What's Holding Things Up?

Mechanization, advanced mechanization, automation, and cybernetics: this is the progression. Most of industry today is in the second phase, while possibly believing itself to be in the third. And automation certainly is within our grasp. what holds it up? You may think what follows is special pleading, but there are observable facts to support the conclusion that management has supposed that because automation is an evolutionary step, it simply arrives as part of the ordinary development in our ways of doing things. But, as a matter of observation, this does not happen, or at least it happens incredibly slowly. Consider the lag between what we know how to do and what our practice actually is. Bright commentators who are well aware of this lag pontificate on television and in the press to tell us what the reason is. They blame the manager—he is stupid, he is old-fashioned, he is complacent, he ought to be sacked. I often think these commentators are so busy writing articles and making broadcasts that they never meet any real-life managers. If they did, they would find that most of them are not like this at all. But why abandon a good theory simply because the facts betray it!

No, the reason why the second Industrial Revolution does not erupt is implicit in the arguments of this book. It depends on the organization and structure of our systems. Why is industry organized as it is? Why do we distinguish between production, sales, engineering, research, and finance? The answer is terribly simple. A modern business is a big and complicated affair. No one man can cope with all of it; the limitations of the human hand, eye, and brain commit us to departmental activity. There is a division of labor even in the highest intellectual flights of endeavor. Some people must specialize in one thing, others in another. The divisions of industry are based on the human limitation fundamentally. They are also concerned with historical and geographical constraint.

The historical constraints have to do with the way that any given firm has actually evolved. It started as a small operation, and grew by accretion. Therefore its anatomy, as we may study it today, is

The inaccuracy of the customary organization chart as a model of a firm is not that it assigns functions to discrete boxes, but that the connections assumed (blue) between the boxes are absurdly naïve. The real lines of communication are more likely to resemble those shown in black.

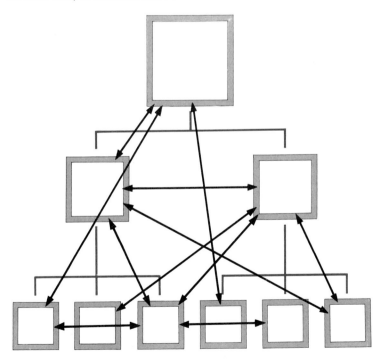

not the result of a logical analysis of what such an anatomy should be; it is a structure frozen out of time. Geographically, too, there is a natural tendency to build management units around the operations in one place; and this holds whether we are talking about two production departments at opposite ends of a single works, or about the home market and the market in another country. But even the frozen history and petrified geography are functions of human limitation, since, without the constraints imposed by the hand, eye, and brain, it would have been possible (historically) to integrate this year's new development into last year's fact in an indivisible whole. And it would be possible to treat India and America as an indivisible market, if the management of the home plant—say in Europe—had instant telepathic knowledge of what was happening at a distance.

So we reach a point in understanding where we see that the way everything is structured really derives from a *human* incapacity to be structured differently. Now automation comes on the scene. Its peripheral equipment gives us the facility to sense things that are going on, and to measure them, on any scale and at any distance. So much for the limitations of human perception, which can accommodate only a little input from short range. Next, automation provides the facility for the very rapid transmission of all these data over any distance, so that they may be collected together, stored, and turned into patterns by a computer. So much for the human limitations on comprehension, which can store and sort and make patterns very cleverly but on a restricted scale again. Finally, automation provides the capability to make choices and to take decisions using all this information, whereas the poor brain finds it difficult to handle more than a few variables at once. At least, it finds it difficult in a quantitative sense. If we need numerical answers, we are quickly beaten by even three variables. I remember demonstrating this to an international congress of savants. I put three linear equations in three variables on a blackboard, and invited those present to solve for x, y, and z in their heads. The coefficients were single digits, and there was a unique solution; but no one could do it.

So the argument runs like this. We have, over the centuries, devised a management structure for running things, whether firms or whole countries. This structure depends absolutely on the limitations of the human hand, eye, and brain. The discoveries of management cybernetics, coupled with the techniques of operational research and with the new technology of automation, make possible a new way of running things, which is not so limited. Yet we insist on retaining the original structures and automating them. In so doing, we enshrine in steel, glass, and semiconductors those very limitations of hand, eye, and brain that the computer was invented precisely to transcend.

Rethinking About Rethinking

Thus it is that when people talk about the need to " rethink " before making a computer application, they rarely mean what I am trying to convey. They rightly believe that the *process* that they are about to automate ought to be gone through with a fine-tooth comb, to see if it can be improved: This is a matter for O & M procedures. But beneath this process lies the problem that this process is intended to solve. It is this that has to be rethought.

For example, I suppose the biggest single class of computer application in the world's industry so far has been the automation of payrolls. Imagine a wage office full of clerks, who are all making complicated calculations. A man's basic wage has to be discovered, and to this must be added any special rates to which he is entitled. Then there is the effect of incentive schemes, which can be exceedingly complicated, and involve a tremendous amount of

The payroll computer shown on the right represents probably the most widespread use of computers in business. It is arguable, however, that the automation of an existing structure (i.e., a separate pay office) may be a less than optimum use of computing potential.

information retrieval. When the gross entitlement has been found, it is necessary to make deductions: for income tax, for various insurance contributions, and perhaps for voluntary payments of other kinds. Well, if computers are as " clever " as people claim, there is no reason why all this should not be automated. There will be a huge saving in clerical effort, and enough money ought to be saved to pay for the computer. It is very likely that it will.

This process, however, whether manual, mechanized, or automated, is intended to solve the problem of rewarding men for their work. But the plant is not what it used to be. In the case I am thinking of, it is highly mechanized, and its output is being monitored by an on-line control computer. This means to say that quite subtle ways could be found for measuring the effort of the workpeople, and for computing its value. No longer need dubious paper-and-ink records be kept, to be sent to an office, there to be translated into punch-card tabulations that look more accurate than they basically are. No longer need the ingenious incentive schemes attempt to provide in advance for all possible situations. The payment of men in this case could be a by-product of the control machinery of the plant itself, of which the labor force is an integral part.

What then *is* a wages office in these circumstances? It has no valid existence. So there is little point in automating it. The reason why it gets automated is that it comes under the office function in the firm. And this function, forgetting that it is a handmaid rather than a profit-earning entity in its own right, is engaged in its own march toward automation —a target that it will reach by hook or by crook.

Meanwhile, out in the works, the production people have enough problems of their own with the on-line control computer. They are quite content to let the office function carry on as before. The problem out here is (to take another particular case) to cut up a long thin bar of hot metal into lengths that can be handled. The customer is ordering these bars in lengths measuring eighteen to twenty-two feet. Now the weight of metal ingot being fed into this process is known only approximately, and so is the proportion of scrap that will have to be chopped off the top and tail of the resulting long bar as it is rolled. Therefore the man in charge of the cutters has little alternative but to set himself to cut fixed lengths, and to hope the piece left over at the end, which is scrap, is not too long. And this could be a high proportion of the total length of the bar. In fact, it represents, on average, a waste of 16 per cent. This is a very great deal, and involves a loss of many hundreds of thousands of dollars a year. For the scrap value of the metal is quite low; the mill is wasting the added value of all the processing that has been done so far.

The cutting has to be done quickly while the metal is hot, and there is no time to measure the full length, still less to calculate how it can best be divided up. But given electronic methods of measurement and the automation of the shearman's skill, it will obviously be possible to eliminate this waste altogether. The computer will choose between alternative possible cuts to take advantage of the four-foot range in requirement. But here comes a complication. Some people do not order their bars to be cut over a range, but to a dead length (plus or minus commercial tolerances alone). In such cases, automation of the cut-up is of no help at all, and waste is still incurred. If the two kinds of order are equally mixed, it may be that installation of the computer is going to save half the previous waste, and that 8 per cent on the average will therefore still be incurred. The saving is quite enough to pay for the necessary computer.

While this is going on, however, there are people over in the sales department worrying about the delivery promises given to various customers. Very likely these people are also installing a computer, to keep track of order progressing and planning. They know, should anyone ask them, that while the works computer is busily cutting up a bar into dead lengths and losing 16 per cent in scrap, the next bar coming along behind—having an identical specification to the previous bar—is intended for someone who wants the 18- to 22-foot range. Unfortunately, there is no way of telling the works computer this, because to do so it would have to have a knowledge of the order book, and the order book belongs to the sales department.

Sales is looking to its own prerogatives. No one in the works has anything to do with the order book, and moreover sales is rather excited by its own progress from manual recording, through mechanization, to automation. The production people are quite content—they want nothing to do with the order book, and it is not their concern. The result is that the works computer remains satisfied with its saving of 8 per cent, whereas it could have had a saving of 16 per cent. Besides, the sales department is fully occupied in discussions with the office people about how invoicing should be done. Sales has the up-to-date progress position in its computer; but the office computer has the *right* to carry on billing people as before, and it has space to use up on its own computer after the payroll job is done.

It is rather tedious. The human beings in these stories are having quite enough trouble trying to automate the processes for which they have always been responsible, without beginning to think about other people's processes. Mark well: These things actually happen, and are going on all around us, although they do not necessarily all happen at once. The general manager of the firm just described would really be rather stupid. But all the separate bits of the composite situation described have actually been observed, and it seems that there is a powerful tendency in industry to go in this direction. This is because it is just another step in the direction industry has always gone.

We must try to learn the lessons of this story. Not only are people failing to rethink the problems that underlie the processes they are automating. They also fail to rethink the structure that underlies the problems. For, as has been strongly argued, the structures that are there are frozen out of space and time; they are not necessarily the right structures for the present world. Of course, there are policies to rethink too, which underlie the structures. And these in turn depend upon the purposes of the firm. How long is it since anyone really thought about those?

Why Not Just Leave Things to Evolve?

We are calling for a very great cerebral effort on the part of management. It is too much, you say. After all, the whole business will gradually evolve to a correct answer, even if some of the installations made on the way are less than fully efficient. But this does not necessarily follow.

Firms do tend to be a little narcissistic. Look how advanced we are, they say: We have automated the payroll, or the cut-up line, or the order book. This in itself puts a brake on the process of rethinking. But there is worse to come. The management is going to find that automation is not all they hoped it would be. The computer to eliminate waste paid for itself; but now people find themselves asked to bear in mind the cost of reprogramming the machine, should they wish to make a change in the wage structure. The computer in the sales department paid for itself; but the storage capacity of the machine has been used up, and the board is asked to buy a larger model before this one has amortized. No one, it is clear, is making a fortune.

Worst of all, the little boxes of management now have vested interests in preserving their identity, and their arguments for doing so are even more difficult to gainsay than they were before. For the process of automating an existing situation somehow reinforces the walls that separate one department from another. It is not difficult to see why this should happen. Accepted management theory is founded on the premise that delegation of responsibility to one box of activities must automatically award absolute authority to the manager concerned. If he is not autonomous (within the company's general policy framework), then he cannot be held responsible. The prospect of automation for this manager, then, is treated by senior management in the usual way. Special services are provided to help him, if he wishes to use them, but the decisions as to what should be done are his alone. Thus it is that the accountant decides how to automate the cost office and the payroll, the production man and the engineer decide how to automate the works, and so on. These consequences sound very sensible, for surely these people know what they are talking about.

The trouble is this. These are the very people who have spent a lifetime learning why things have to be as they are. They are, in this sense, the very last people to consider how things should be altered. Moreover, the social conventions of the firm make it a solecism for these men to enter into negotiations with counterparts in other activities: Everyone is supposed to get on with the thing he knows about. And so the great new technology of automation has no means of expressing its potential, and management never appreciates how to exploit it.

I do not want to be misquoted on this matter. It does not follow from these arguments that it is always wrong to supply new lamps for old. Many existing computer applications and other examples of automation are very well worth while, and we must be influenced by the argument that people have to find out how these machines work. But it is possible to ask for a parallel activity to this orthodox development activity. There should be constant study of the possibilities opened up by automation, and this is a matter from which senior management must opt out. Very often they do: They declare that it is a technical matter, fit for electronic engineers and experts in data processing. But anyone who has followed the general arguments of this book on the matter of the indivisibility of viable systems will surely recognize that automation provides a heaven-sent opportunity to recreate the integral management that the firm enjoyed a century ago, before the gaffer found the enterprise too big for him, and broke it into fragments. We have become very clever in organizing a fragmented company to work as if it were integral. But given an opportunity actually to put the pieces together again, we must seize it. Otherwise we shall get what might be called rational but trivial automation.

The alternative is simple enough in concept, but needs courage to contemplate. Remember the call, to rethink the purposes of the firm, and then the policies that interpret these purposes. After this, structures appropriate to the implementation of these policies must be worked out, and the problems to which such structures give rise elucidated. Only then do we reach the processes involved in solving the problems, and the question whether automation is the answer. Given this call as a raw statement, it would not be surprising if the typical manager went white. How on earth is he to approach this gigantic task, given that he is already fully occupied in running a successful business?

The answer is to take the raw statement in context. We have been talking about management science, which is well adapted through operational research and cybernetics to embark on this very exercise. It is not a question of sitting down with a wet towel around one's head. A model of the company and its activity is needed, and we have seen how this may be given substance. Indeed, it is not necessary to say anything about automation at all. If we use

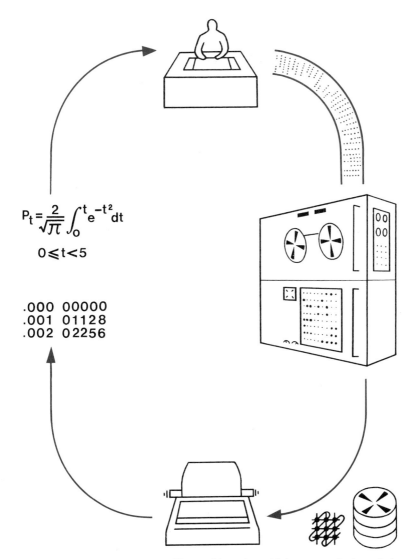

$$P_t = \frac{2}{\sqrt{\pi}} \int_0^t e^{-t^2} dt$$

$$0 \leqslant t < 5$$

```
.000 00000
.001 01128
.002 02256
```

A simple use of a computer. The problem, for which a numerical result is required, is given to a programmer, who prepares the problem in machine language; the resulting " program " is fed to the computer, which may print the results on a teleprinter or use them automatically in some further process.

management science to make an analysis of the nature of the firm and its activity, these questions about purposes, policies, and the rest will be entertained. And naturally, if the interdisciplinary group is competent, it will know very well what facilities automation can offer toward improvement in the firm's affairs.

Thus automation should be stumbled upon by accident in the routine process of modern management. This is a very different proposition from those normally encountered. How do we use a computer? This question is as unprofessional in my ears as the equivalent question: How do we use linear programming? It is as if a painter produced a perfectly lovely portrait, admired by all, but there was no sitter for it; and the artist spends years carrying the painting around from place to place looking for someone so like his picture that he can sell it. Ten to one, also, when one does find the perfect situation for automation or for the use of an operational research technique, the management will already have discovered the perfect answer without the use of either.

Many examples could be given of the muddle we are getting ourselves into. Unfortunately, people who should know better sometimes take the line of least resistance. Thus it happens that one of the most important computer companies in the world is advertising its machines with the statement: " You won't have to redesign procedures or change the contents of your reports, invoices, or other documents." The advertisers are ill-advised. There may be a short-term payoff from this approach, but in the longer term these protagonists of automation must be defeating their own ends. The same can be said of those who undertake the application of automation piecemeal. Not only do they incur the penalties already enumerated here; they also create a social problem that is really a result of this lack of insight. If the object of automation is seen—quite erroneously—as a means of replacing men by machines, then big problems of human redundancy will naturally arise. But they are not discussed here, for they are bogus. The job to do is to increase the national product, not to throw men out of work; and given proper management science this job can be done.

We'll-Learn-in-Time Diehards
Before closing this discussion, it is worth remarking that the

whole battery of arguments developed here applies just as well to other kinds of business, and to government itself, as to the individual firm. Take any example you like, and try out the arguments. Here are one or two illustrations. In banking we find a system frozen in time and space if there ever was one. Whenever an ordinary customer wants to make use of a bank's facilities, he finds the building shut. The whole business of banking is decentralized into localities, on the understanding that there is no way of acquiring information from the center—which of course there now is. Thus, despite the well-known fact that there are not enough bank managers to go around, processes of further centralization are taking a long time to achieve. This is because the task is regarded as one of linking branches together into a centralized network, instead of a task of rethinking the purposes of the bank. Again, consider the use of personal checks. These cannot yet be read directly by machine, because we all write so badly, but modernity suggests that the information they contain should be processed by machine. Therefore it has been thought a sensible idea to recreate the check in formalized characters, using magnetic ink so that machines can read them after all. In order to avoid the need for a man to read the check, a man reads the check to put it on a machine so that the machine can read the check. It is all very unsatisfactory. One banker, challenged with all this and more besides, was hurt that he was regarded as reactionary. He declared with evident pride that a young accountant had just been appointed to examine the entire operations of his bank with a view to their automation: " And," he added, " in case you should think that we lightly regard this as an easy task, you should know that the man has been told that no report is expected for fifteen years." One could almost hear the mental afterthought: " By then, thank God, I shall have retired."

It is a shame to pick on banks for such rude treatment, because there are many business activities of which the same is true. All the operations of insurance and finance deal, like banking, with information as the only important raw material. They are preeminently suited to the kind of analysis proposed in this book, and to sensible uses of automation. But the public is still exposed to a situation in which the documents involved in any transactions in

The Decca Automatic Navigation Display in this airliner flight deck not only automatically computes the aircraft's position continuously, but also displays the result on a map for the pilots.

these informational processing industries are incomprehensible except to experts, and in which there are terrible delays, frustrations, and uncertainties. If these businesses are in fact competitive, as is claimed, then the company that moves first towards a genuinely scientific answer should sweep the board.

Passing from private enterprise, we reach an area that is in most countries public enterprise—the provision of general services such as travel. Here again we see the fallacies of compartmentalization committed by the individual firm reproduced on a large scale. The system of transportation is not coherent; it is not treated as integral. Roads compete with railroads and airlines in chaotic fashion, and at immense cost to the nation. These individual modes of transport are themselves treated in a divisionalized and localized way, as if it meant something to say that a piece of a railroad system, for example, were profitable or unprofitable and could be improved or abandoned accordingly. As the occupancy of an airline falls, and it needs more money, the price of tickets rises—thereby improving the chances of successful competition from road or rail. Meanwhile, the scientific effort at the disposal of such enterprises is frittered away in the improvement and perhaps automation of processes that perhaps should never be undertaken. This is not management science at all.

When we come to government itself, the situation is even worse. A health service or an education service, for example, unfolds its checkered career, moving from crisis to crisis in every advanced country in the world. Examination of purposes is restricted to the elevated discussion of liberal principles; it is not undertaken in the practical context of affairs. I was once responsible for the effective use of a highly concentrated and very specialized educational unit concerned with improving literacy in a matter of eight weeks. It was accepted that criteria were needed by which to exclude from this facility such candidates as had already attained a standard beyond that for which the course was provided. But the attempt to introduce criteria to help in deciding which candidates were too *retarded* to have a chance of benefiting from the course was achieved only after the bloodiest of battles. " No man is in-educable," was the liberal cry. No doubt: But in the world of practical management one surely must acknowledge that there are people who are effectively ineducable given eight weeks in which to do the job.

It is strange how the " practical men " charged with the responsibility for managing affairs often turn out to be very unrealistic. The management scientist, whom the practical man will often label impractical by definition, seeks to measure the resources available before finding a means for their optimal allocation to desirable objectives. Thus a health service must have enough doctors and an educational service must have enough teachers. If there are not enough of either (and in Great Britain today this is the case), management has two courses open to it. Either it can improve pay and conditions, and thereby attract a larger staff, or it must use modern approaches—such as automation—to eke out the facilities it has. This means bringing operational research into the organization of general practice, for example, regardless of whether this would seem to intervene in the doctor's Hippocratic understanding with his patient or not.

It might be better to receive a prescription " inhumanly " from a computer, than to die for lack of medicine. It might be better to be taught arithmetic " like a battery hen " by the world's best teacher on television, than to spend one's time playing naughts and crosses at the back of a class of forty students supervised by an incompetent. In fact, the alternatives open are not as bad as these. Operational research could undoubtedly devise means of diagnosis and innocuous treatment for a range of mild disorders without bothering the skilled medical man. Cybernetics could undoubtedly design teaching machines achieving much more rapport with the pupil than an unresponsive television screen. But governments do not invest in either of these things. They prefer to believe that everything will eventually turn out all right if they exhibit sufficient political skill. But the needs are measurable, and grow rapidly. And the resources are measurable too, and grow little, if at all. The system of interaction involved may be quantified with a model, and the outcome is demonstrably disastrous. Humanistic beliefs and political promises are irrelevant to factual situations of this kind, and the people who embrace them are mystics.

If we say that problems such as these can be tackled scientifically, we are not invoking an equal mysticism of another sort, as some contend. Science is not a magic word, and scientists are not demigods. On the other hand, science enshrines the codified knowledge that mankind has about the universe, and scientific method sums up mankind's experience in the rational approach to problems. Must it be thought an overstatement of the case, must it be overselling, to preach with all the passion at one's command that really difficult problems deserve professional treatment?

Death of a Diehard

This book has argued that huge, not meager, savings and improvements are made possible by the integral control of integral systems. The case has been put by philosophy, by the analysis of what life is actually like, and by many examples of actual achievements. It is necessary that people with the power should act, at every level of management.

The ultimate in automation: These secondary-school pupils are being taught computer programming by automatic, feedback-controlled teaching machines.

By the turn of the century, cataclysm apart, the population of this earth will have doubled. The management problems that attend this fact in every sphere and at every level are almost unthinkably great. Models from biology of evolutionary processes superficially lend support to those who think that answers will inevitably propose themselves: It will all come right. But let us undertake a little exploration down the cone of resolution for adaptive systems, see what the subsystems are, and what a paleontological mapping of " it will all come right " looks like. The dinosaurs thought so too.

Index

Note: Numbers in italics refer to illustrations and captions to illustrations.